World Peace is something we all want.

Ending world hunger is a worthy goal.

So is helping under-developed countries find success.

The question is –

How should we go about pursuing all this?

America.

Why did people come from distant shores, risk a dangerous journey, come to a raw and undeveloped country.

Freedom –
They were willing to fight and yes
– even risk dying – to keep it.

What we have is so strong and sustainable that emigrants continue to come, looking for the same freedom, individual rights, and opportunities that brought our forefathers.

EXCEPTIONAL PROFILE OF COURAGE

*The United Nations
vs.
American Liberty*

Al Snow, Sr.

Exceptional Profile of Courage:
    The United Nations vs. American Liberty
By Al Snow, Sr.

© 2002 by Al Snow, Sr.
First Edition

All Rights Reserved. No part of this book may be reproduced in any manner whatsoever without the written permission of the author, except in the case of brief quotations in reviews and articles.

All Government Documents contained herein are Public Domain. Italics are added for emphasis.

Publisher's Cataloging-in-Publication
(Provided by Quality Books, Inc.)

Snow, Al.
    Exceptional profile of courage : The United Nations vs American liberty / Al Snow, Sr. -- 1st ed.
    p.cm.
    Includes index
    LCCN: 2002106135
    ISBN: 1888106646

    1. Civil rights--United States. 2. United Nations--United States. 3. Liberty. I. Title.

JC599.U5S66   323'.0973
                                  QBI02-200366

Printed in the United States of America
Cover Design Lea Taylor

Agreka™ LLC
800 360-5284
www.agreka.com

Dedication

*To my twenty-three grandchildren
and to all those who may come later.
May you know by my actions that there is no doubt
I love my Country, its Constitution, and its sovereignty.*

Table of Contents

Introduction	9
Articles of Confederation Excerpts	19
Republic vs. Democracy	22
Preamble of the Constitution	24
Bill of Rights Excerpts	25

Chapter 1 U.S. Military Personnel and the U.N. — 27
A Questionnaire Presented to 300 U.S. Marines

Chapter 2 "The American's Creed" — 34
Accepted by the House of Representatives on behalf of all American citizens on April 3, 1918

Chapter 3 Why a U.N.-Free Zone Ordinance? — 45

Chapter 4 Evaluation of the UN-Free Ordinance by Herbert W. Titus, a Legal Advisor to Congressman Ron Paul (R-Texas) — 55

Chapter 5 Pertinent Facts About the United Nations — 59

Chapter 6 U.N. Declared a Sovereign World Government, 1970 — 66

Chapter 7 It All Began with The League of Nations Events 1916 thru 1935 — 70

Chapter 8 Birth of the United Nations 1945 — 75

Chapter 9 How the U.S. Would Interact with the U.N. "U.N. Participation Act of 1945" — 80

Chapter 10 Proposals for New Disarmament Program Speech by John F. Kennedy to U.N., 1961 — 91

Chapter 11	"Freedom from War – the United States Program for General and Complete Disarmament in a Peaceful World." 1961 U.S. Dept of State Publication 7277.	104
Chapter 12	Review of "Arms Control and Disarmament Act" Public Law 87-297	120
Chapter 13	Text of – "Arms Control and Disarmament Act" Public Law 87-297	125
Chapter 14	The Solution Proposed in 2001 H.R. 1146 The American Sovereignty Restoration Act By Congressman Ron Paul (R-Texas)	139
Chapter 15	Conclusion	169
About the Author		175
Acknowledgments		177
Biosphere Reserve & World Heritage Sites		181
United Nations Agencies and Other International Organizations, Conventions, Resolutions and Treaties		184
Definitions of Rights & Powers Within the United States Constitution		187
Glossary		194
Index		209
Contact Information		221

Introduction

The question every thinking American needs to ask – Is there an entangling alliance with the United Nations that can never be untangled? How will it serve the United States in the years to come. *And each individual American.* The United States has one vote among 191 nations. One.

A growing number of concerned Americans believe we are relinquishing what our forefathers held so dear. They see that in our effort to cooperate with the UN, we are giving away – piece by piece – the freedoms to govern our own personal lives.

As a U.S. citizen, you need to become aware of the gradual transfer of U.S. decision-making power – military, environmental, economic, labor, arms control, and taxing – to the United Nations.

Much good has been accomplished by the United Nations in its 56 year history, and many countries and their peoples have benefited. What we wish to address in this book is how the U.N. Charter, amendments, activities, and goals have slowly but steadily become entangled with the individual freedoms guaranteed every U.S. citizen in the Constitution and Bill of Rights.

Many less powerful countries do not have the resources of America. They have nothing to lose and everything to gain from transferring their sovereignty to the U.N.

Al Snow, Sr.

> The United States should not withdraw from the world. It can establish individual Treaties with other countries, and still keep its sovereignty. As a major world power, it can continue to interact in the ways it chooses so that individual American rights can be preserved.

Everywhere I go, I'm asked, "Why in the world would a town board or a city council pass an ordinance making their community a U.N.–Free Zone?" To answer this question, one must gain an understanding of the sweeping changes proposed by the United Nations for all nations of the world.

> People are being led to believe that in order to live in an *interdependent* world, all nations and states within nations must yield their sovereignty to a one world government (the United Nations).

If you have been unaware of all that has transpired with the UN, you can remedy this by reading and pondering the material we provide herein, which includes extensive legal document excerpts (now public domain).

> We owe it to our ancestors and the Founding Fathers to educate ourselves and form our own opinion.

You will learn how the U.S. began with the Articles of Confederation, which then led to the writing of the Constitution – and why. You'll learn how the United Nations came to be – and why. We list the changes made to the United Nations Charter and the events that brought these changes to pass.

Many well meaning people have believed U.N. plans are good for the world. But have they really looked at the accompanying gradual erosion of the rights of individual Americans:

> In a speech to the nation and the world on September 11, 1990, the senior and former president Bush stated "Out of these troubled times, our fifth objective – a new

world order – can emerge." A few days later on September 17, 1990, *Time* magazine noted a comment by Senior Bush, who said "... would like to make the United Nations a cornerstone of its plans to construct a New World Order."

As you read the material we present, you will begin to see what so many other Americans now see.

The question to ask yourself: Am I willing to relinquish my individual freedoms – and those of my children – for the global plans of the United Nations.

And, by the way, who has the power to make those decisions for you. Can the national government make them for The People, or make them in behalf of the individual states of the Union. Can your state make that decision for you. Or does the U.S. Constitution and your state constitution prohibit such actions. And if so, why are they being made.

How many "good laws" have been passed in this country that later came back to bite us with results no one anticipated. Yet, they are now the law of the land.

Read the agenda presented by the Council of Global Government, which met at the United Nations in New York City the summer of 2001, to amend the United Nations Charter. Their agenda may sound good on first reading, but read deeper and ponder how they could eventually affect you and your family. And those yet unborn. These are but more steps added to the many that have already been taken over the past 56 years.

Twelve Principles Presented in 2001 to be Amended to
the United Nations Charter –

Principle 1: Calls for the consolidation of all international agencies under direct United Nations authority.

Principle 2: Calls for regulation by the United Nations of all transnational corporations and financial institutions, requiring an "International Code of Conduct" concerning environment and labor standards.

Principle 3: Demands an independent source of revenue for the U. N, such as the Tobin Tax, taxes on aircraft and shipping fuels, and licensing of Global Commons, defined as "outer space" atmosphere, non-territorial seas, and related environment that supports life. This paves the way for other type global taxes.

Principle 4: Eliminates veto power and permanent membership status on the Security Council.

Principle 5: Authorizes a standing United Nations army.

Principle 6: Requires United Nations registration of all arms and reduction of all national armies as "part of a multilateral global security system" under the authority of the United Nations.

Principal 7: Requires individual and national compliance with all United Nations "Human Rights" treaties and declarations.

Principle 8: Activates the International Criminal Court (ICC), making the International Court of Justice compulsory for all nations and gives individuals the right to petition courts to remedy social justices. Every individual will be subject to the ICC.

Principle 9: Calls for a new institution to establish economic and environmental security by insuring "sustainable development."

Principle 10: Calls for the establishment of an International Environmental Court.

Principle 11: Calls for the declaration that climate change is an essential global security interest that requires the creation of a "high-level action team" to allocate carbon emission based on equal per capita rights.

Principle 12: Calls for the cancellation of all debt owed by the poorest nations, global poverty reductions, and for equitable sharing of global resources as allocated by the United Nations.

Some legal scholars believe these 12 principles, and others the U.N. has passed and hope to pass, set a precedent that will eventually lead to the following –

- An end to individual rights guaranteed by the U.S. Constitution: freedom of religion, freedom of speech, freedom of the press, freedom of assembly, the right to trial by jury, and the right to keep and bear arms, etc.

- National and personal disarmament, along with *conscription* of U.S. citizens into a United Nations Army or Police Force.

- The end of private property rights and the ability to control our own home, farm or business.

- Loss of our right as parents to raise and instruct our children in accordance with our personal beliefs.

- Population control measures that determine when, how many, or if we can have children.

- U.S. economic and environmental regulation by the U.N.

- Global taxation.

- A centrally managed world monetary system.

- Environmental controls that could mean the end of single family homes and personal automobile ownership.

Americans unknowingly ask – But, doesn't the United Nations just deal with international issues.

Does it become a local issue if the United Nations can take your right to private ownership of property, tell you how many children you can have, mandate what you can teach your children, tell you where you can live and not live, tax you with a global tax, take your gun or guns?

George Washington stated in his farewell address: "The great rule of conduct for us, in regard to foreign nations, is, in extending our commercial relations, to have with them as little *political connection* as possible."

Thomas Jefferson stated, "...essential principles" of our nation; "...peace, commerce, and honest friendship with all nations, *entangling alliances with none.*"

Yes, there is an entangling alliance and yes, it can be untangled. However, we need to do it now while the U.S. still has its sovereignty. If the U.S. yields its sovereignty to a one-world government, then it will be impossible.

The authority to govern this nation is derived *from the people,* not the national government. Power flows upward not down.

Samuel Adams stated: "If ye love wealth greater than liberty, the tranquillity of servitude greater than the animating contest for freedom, go home from us in peace. We seek not your counsel, nor your arms. Crouch down and lick the hand that feeds you; and may posterity forget that ye were our countrymen."

Because we believe that each town and city in the U.S. is slowly losing its constitutional protections to Washington, who is giving it to the United Nations, my hometown, LaVerkin, Utah, has taken preventative action.

> The LaVerkin City Council has passed a United Nations Free Zone ordinance, to make a statement that shapes the public debate and forces the people of LaVerkin, Utah, and the rest of the country to educate themselves. And the hoped for result is that people were shocked

16 JAN 2002 Repealed

Exceptional Profile of Courage

and are now interested in learning about the U.N. Charter and the U.N. Statute of the International Court of Justice. I have yet to meet a single person in LaVerkin who had read the U.N. Charter before the U.N.–Free Zone Ordinance was passed.

LaVerkin is nestled in a beautiful valley at the foot of Zion National Park with its tall mountains, rugged cliffs, and painted rocks. In the southwest corner of Utah at an elevation of 3,266 feet, it is 25 miles from St. George and the Arizona border.

Of particular interest to those who live near wilderness areas –

There are 47 or more Biosphere Reserves and 20 or more World Heritage sites occupying over 50 million acres of United States soil at the present time, under partial control of the U.N. and all done without a local vote. (see Biosphere Reserves & World Heritage).

Yellowstone National Park, for example: Of the $20.00 fee to enter the Park – part of that fee goes to the United Nations. The U. S. government agreed to limit its right of sovereignty over these lands by deferring to international mandates promoted by the United Nations through their International Inter-Governmental Organizations, and non-Governmental Organizations.

Executive Order (EO) 12986 was signed by Bill Clinton on January 19, 1996.

Most U.S. citizens have never heard of EO12986, and fewer U.S. citizens could identify the IUCN or explain why it merits such privileged treatment by President Clinton's Executive Order.

The IUCN is one of the U.N.'s major agencies in creating and implementing global environmental policy.

The IUCN is an accredited scientific advisory body to the United

Nations and has more than 880 state and federal government agency and non-governmental organization members in 133 countries. In 1993 the IUCN received over 1.2 million dollars in U.S. tax money by way of the U.S. State Department.

> LaVerkin City gets some of its water supply from the Virgin River, which starts in Zion National Park. There is a possibility that the United Nations could be given a biosphere within the boundary of Zion Park, which could affect our ability to irrigate our crops, fields, trees, gardens and yards.

Few U.S. citizens are aware that the U.N. International Criminal Court (ICC) would like to replace the American Court system. The ICC would have the ability to reach in and rework a nation's moral, family, social, and community standards to correspond to the requirements of the United Nations.

> In April, 12, 2002, *The Salt Lake Tribune* article, "World Court Comes Into Force Despite U.S. Refusal to Ratify," by Edith M. Lederer, The Associated Press, reported, "The world's first permanent war crimes tribunal got the necessary international backing Thursday to come into force July 1 ... hailed by human rights activists and many nations but strongly opposed by the United States....Pierre-Richard Prosper, the U.S. ambassador for war crimes, restated President Bush's opposition to the treaty and refusal to ratify it. The United States fears American citizens would be subject to frivolous or politically motivated prosecutions.... 'The goal is noble and we agree with the goal of accountability.... What we disagree with is this precise mechanism for putting this goal in place,' Prosper said. ... 'The prosecutor and a handful of judges could make a political decision to prosecute a U.S. official or serviceman. This is a possibility we take seriously,' Prosper said."

Few U.S. citizens are aware of U.S. Department of State publication 7277 called "Freedom from War – the United States Program for General and Complete Disarmament in a Peaceful World" (1961), based on the plan presented to the U.N. by John F. Kennedy in 1961. Read his speech to the U.N., then a review of this document, and the document itself.

Today, the United Nations is vocal about its desire to govern people of all nations. You may ask, How could this possibly come about? Let's take a look at Henry Kissinger's address at the Bilderbergers meeting in Evian, France, on May 21, 1992.

> "Today Americans would be outraged if U.N. troops entered Los Angeles to restore order; tomorrow they will be grateful! This is especially true if they were told there was an outside threat from beyond whether real or promulgated, that threatened our very existence. It is then that all peoples of the world will plead with world leaders to deliver them from this evil. The one thing every man fears is the unknown. When presented with this scenario, individual rights will be willingly relinquished for the guarantee of their well being granted to them by their world government."

The development of a U.N. world "police force" might be the act that awakens every U.S. citizen.

Everyone of us in the U.S. need to encourage our fellow Americans to better understand and appreciate the principles of good government that are set forth in our Nation's founding documents. They protect what you want protected.

Action is being taken. Congressman Ron Paul (R-Texas) re-introduced HR 1146, "American Sovereignty Restoration Act of 2001" on March 21, 2001. The two cosponsors are: Bob Stump (R-Ariz) and Richard Pombo (R-Calif).

We must become an informed nation. And that is the purpose of this book.

Al Snow, Sr.

To begin, we want to gain your immediate attention. Chapter One contains a recent questionnaire that the U.S. government required 300 United States Marines to answer about their possible future involvement with the U.N. as military personnel.

Once you read this, you will want to know more.

But first read excerpts of The Articles of Confederation, the first legal document that governed our country. As you learn where the country has been, you will better understand where it is going. We also address what a Republic really is, and then excerpts of the Bill of Rights.

As you encounter various terms of which you are unfamiliar, see Definitions and Glossary, and Rights & Powers within the United States Constitution, and their definitions.

Articles of Confederation,
first constitution of the United States.

(Excerpts)
The Articles were in force from March 1, 1781, to June 21, 1788, when the present Constitution of the United States went into effect. The Articles were written in 1777 during the early part of the American Revolution by a committee of the Second Continental Congress of the 13 colonies.

The head of the committee, John Dickinson, presented a report on the proposed articles to the Congress on July 12, 1776, eight days after the signing of the Declaration of Independence. Dickinson *initially proposed a strong central government*, with control over the western lands, equal representation for the states, and the power to levy taxes.

Because of their experience with Great Britain, the 13 states feared a powerful central government; consequently, they changed Dickinson's proposed articles drastically before they sent them to all the states for ratification in November 1777.

The Continental Congress had been careful to give the states as much independence as possible and to specify the limited functions of the federal government. Despite these precautions, several years passed before all the states ratified the articles. The delay resulted from preoccupation with the revolution and from disagreements among the states....

These disagreements included quarrels over boundary lines, conflicting decisions by state courts, differing tariff laws, and trade restrictions between states. The small states wanted equal representation with the large states in Congress, and the large states were afraid they would have to pay an excessive amount of money to support the federal government. In addition, the states disagreed over control of the western territories. The states with no frontier borders wanted the government to control the sale of these territories so that all the states profited. On the other hand, the states bordering the frontier wanted to control as much land as they could. Eventually the states agreed to give control of all western lands to the federal government, paving the way for final ratification of the articles on March 1, 1781.

II. The Provisions of the Articles

The articles created a loose confederation of independent states that gave *limited powers* to a central government. The national government would consist of a single house of Congress, where each state would have one vote. Congress had the power to set up a postal department, to estimate the costs of the government and request donations from the states, to raise armed forces, and to control the development of the western territories. With the consent of nine of the thirteen states, Congress could also coin, borrow, or appropriate money as well as declare war and enter into treaties and alliances with foreign nations.

There was no independent executive and no veto of legislation. Judicial proceedings in each state were to be honored by all other states. The federal government had no judicial branch, and the only judicial authority Congress had was the power to arbitrate disputes between states. Congress was denied the power to levy taxes; the new federal government was financed by donations from the states based on the value of each state's lands. Any amendment to the articles required the unanimous approval of all 13 states.

III. Weaknesses

In attempting to limit the power of the central government, the Second Continental Congress created one without sufficient power to govern effectively, which led to serious national and international problems.

Exceptional Profile of Courage

The greatest weakness of the federal government under the Articles of Confederation was its inability to regulate trade and levy taxes. Sometimes the states refused to give the government the money it needed, and they engaged in tariff wars with one another, almost paralyzing interstate commerce. The government could not pay off the debts it had incurred during the revolution, including paying soldiers who had fought in the war and citizens who had provided supplies to the cause. Congress could not pass needed measures because they lacked the nine-state majority required to become laws. The states largely ignored Congress, which was powerless to enforce cooperation, and it was therefore unable to carry out its duties.

Congress could not force the states to adhere to the terms of the Treaty of Paris of 1783 ending the American Revolution, which was humiliating to the new government, especially when some states started their own negotiations with foreign countries. In addition, the new nation was unable to defend its borders from British and Spanish encroachment because it could not pay for an army when the states would not contribute the necessary funds. Leaders like Alexander Hamilton of New York and James Madison of Virginia criticized the limits placed on the central government, and General George Washington is said to have complained that the federation was "little more than a shadow without substance."

On February 21, 1787, Congress called for a Constitutional Convention to be held in May to revise the articles. Between May and September, the convention wrote the present Constitution of the United States, which retained some of the features of the Articles of Confederation but gave considerably more power to the federal government. It provided for an executive branch and allowed the government to tax its citizens. Congress also went from one house to two houses – the Senate and House of Representatives.

Republic vs. Democracy

The United States is a mixture of two systems of government (Republican under Common Law, and democratic under statutory law). The People enjoy their God-given natural rights in the Republic. In a democracy, the Citizens enjoy only government granted (civil rights) privileges.

The word "democracy" has been popularly used among American citizens for many years. It is now time for everyone to become aware, as did our Forefathers, of the distinction between our Republic and a democracy. It has great legal significance.

The Constitution guarantees to every state a *republican form of government* (Art. 4, Sec. 4). No state may join the United States unless it is a Republic. A Republic is one dedicated to "liberty and justice for all."

Minority individual rights are the priority.

The people have natural rights instead of civil rights. The people are protected by the Bill of Rights from the majority. One vote in a jury can stop all of the majority from depriving any one of the people of his rights; this would not be so if the United States were a democracy.

Read the Pledge of Allegiance:
"I pledge allegiance to the flag of the United States of America, and to the **Republic** for which it stands, one

Nation under God, indivisible, with liberty and justice for all."

In a pure democracy form of government, 51% beats 49%. In a democracy there is no such thing as a significant minority. There are no minority rights except civil rights (privileges) granted by a majority. Simply stated, a pure democracy would be a dictatorship by the majority.

In a Democracy, the sovereignty is in the *whole* body of the free citizens. The sovereignty is not divided to smaller units such as individual citizens. To solve a problem, only the whole body is authorized to act. Also, being citizens, individuals have duties and obligations to the government. The government's only obligations to the citizens are those legislatively pre-defined for it by the whole body politic.

In a Republic, the sovereignty resides in the people themselves, whether one or many. In a Republic, one may act on his own or through his representatives as he chooses to solve a problem. Also, the people have no obligation to the government; instead, the government being hired by the people, is obliged to its owner, the people. The people own the government agencies. The government agencies own the citizens.

In the United States we have a three-tiered system consisting of 1) people, 2) government agencies 3) and citizens.

The people did "ordain and establish this Constitution," not for themselves, but "for the United States of America." In delegating powers to the government agencies the people gave up none of their own. (See Preamble of U.S. Constitution). The adoption of this concept is why the U.S. has been called the *"Great Experiment in self government."* The People govern themselves, while their agents (government agencies) perform tasks listed in the Preamble for the benefit of the People.

Preamble of the Constitution

"We the people of the United States, in order to form a more perfect union, establish justice, insure domestic tranquility, provide for the common defense, promote the general welfare, and secure the blessings of liberty to ourselves and our posterity, do ordain and establish this Constitution for the United States of America."

"If a nation expects to be ignorant and free, in a state of civilization, it expects what never was and never will be." Thomas Jefferson, 1816.

Bill of Rights

Several centuries of English legal tradition, recorded in documents such as the Magna Carta of 1215, the Petition of Right of 1628, and the English Bill of Rights of 1689, contributed to the American Bill of Rights.

(Excerpts)
I. Introduction
Bill of Rights, first ten amendments to the Constitution of the United States. The Bill of Rights establishes basic American civil liberties that the government cannot violate. The states ratified the Bill of Rights in 1791, three years after the Constitution was ratified. Originally the Bill of Rights applied only to the federal government, but in a series of 20th-century cases, the Supreme Court decided that most of its provisions apply to the states. Many countries have used the Bill of Rights as a model for defining civil liberties in their constitutions.

II. Rights Protected
The Bill of Rights includes a wide range of protections with a common theme and purpose – to define the scope of individual freedom in the United States. They are not the only rights contained in the Constitution. But as a group the rights provided in the first ten amendments are the cornerstones of the republic type of government in the United States.

First Amendment
Congress shall make no law respecting an establishment of religion, or prohibiting the free exercise thereof; or abridging the freedom of speech, or of the press, or the right of the people peaceably to assemble, and to petition the Government for a redress of grievances.

Second Amendment
A well regulated Militia, being necessary to the security of a free State, the right of the people to keep and bear Arms, shall not be infringed.

Fourth Amendment
The right of the people to be secure in their persons, houses, papers, and effects, against unreasonable searches and seizures, shall not be violated, and no Warrants shall issue, but upon probable cause, supported by Oath or affirmation, and particularly describing the place to be searched, and the persons or things to be seized.

Ninth Amendment
The enumeration in the Constitution, of certain rights, shall not be construed to deny or disparage others retained by the people.

Tenth Amendment
The powers not delegated to the United States by the Constitution, nor prohibited by it to the States, are reserved to the States respectively, or to the people.

Chapter 1
U.S. Military Personnel and the U.N.
A Questionnaire Presented to 300 U.S. Marines

In the U.S. Code Title 18 – Crimes and Criminal Procedure, 1994 Edition Vol. 9 Subsection 2382, Misprision of Treason states as follows:

> Whoever, owing allegiance to the United States and having knowledge of the commission of any treason against them, conceals and does not, as soon as may be, disclose and make known the same to the President or to some judge of the United States, or to the governor or to some judge or justice of a particular State, is guilty of Misprision of Treason and shall be *fined* under this title *or imprisoned* not more than seven years or both.

(June 25, 1948, Ch. 645, 62 STAT. 807; Sept 13, 1994, Pub. L. 103-322 Title XXXIII Subsection 330016 (1) (H), 108 STAT. 2147.)

AMENDMENTS
1994 – Pub. L. 103-322 substituted "fine under this title" for "fine not more than $1,000."

CROSS REFERENCES
Federal retirement benefits, forfeiture upon conviction of offenses under this section, see section 8312 of Title 5, Government Organization and Employees.

Forfeiture of veterans' benefits upon conviction under this section, see section 6105 of Title 38, Veteran's Benefits.

Al Snow, Sr.

Subsection 2384 Seditious Conspiracy states as follows:

If two or more persons in any State or Territory, or in any place subject to the jurisdiction of the United States, conspire to overthrow, put down, or to destroy by force the Government of the United States, or to levy war against them, or to oppose by force the authority thereof, or by force to prevent, hinder, or delay the execution of any law of the United States, or by force to seize, take, or possess any property of the United States contrary to the authority thereof, they shall each be fined not more than $20,000 or imprisoned not more than twenty years or both. (June 25, 1948, Ch. 645, Subsection 1, 62 STAT. 808; July 24, 1956 Ch. 678, Subsection 1, 70 STAT. 623).

The United Nations Loyalty Oath

"I solemnly swear to exercise in all loyalty, discretion and conscience, the functions entrusted to me as a member of international service of the United Nations; to discharge those functions and regulate *with the interest of the United Nations only in view*, and not to seek or accept instructions in regard to the performance of my duty, from *any government or authority external to the Organization*."

"There is a revolution built into that document,"said ex-Senator William E. Jenner (R-Indiana 1947-1959) regarding the United Nations Charter.

The above oath is evidence that all those who have affiliations with the United Nations, *whether or not also employed in the service of the United States Government*, whenever there is a conflict, must always place their loyalty to the United Nations above the loyalty to the United States.

The question we need to consider:
By taking the U.N. Loyalty Oath, does the U.S. soldier, Congressman, or police officer commit Misprision of Treason when prior to this U.N. Oath they have taken the United States Oath to uphold and protect the United States Constitution?

Exceptional Profile of Courage

I have an UNCLASSIFIED copy of "Peacekeeping and U.N. Operational Control. A Study of Their Effect on Unit Cohesion." Naval Postgraduate School, Monterey, CA, March, 1995.

In the Introduction of this manual it states:
> Unit *cohesion* is historically recognized as the single most critical element in an effective combat fighting force.

On Page 100 – 104 in the unclassified copy described above, the following questions were to be answered by 300 United States Marines. I received this copy from an ex-Marine now living in Texas. In particular, take notice of the last part.

QUESTIONNAIRE EXCERPTS

Do you feel that *U.S. combat troops* should be used in other countries, *under command of non-U.S. officers appointed by the United Nations* for any of the following missions?

24. Drug Enforcement

Strongly disagree/ Disagree / Agree / Strongly Agree–No opinion

25. Disaster relief (e.g. hurricanes, floods, fires, earthquakes)

Strongly disagree/ Disagree / Agree / Strongly Agree–No opinion

26. Environmental disaster clean-up

Strongly disagree/ Disagree / Agree / Strongly Agree–No opinion

27. Peace keeping

Strongly disagree/ Disagree / Agree / Strongly Agree–No opinion

28. National building (Reconstruct civil government, develop public school System, develop or improve public transportation system, etc.)

Strongly disagree/ Disagree / Agree / Strongly Agree–No opinion

29. Humanitarian relief (food and medical supplies, temporary housing, and Clothing)

Strongly disagree/ Disagree / Agree / Strongly Agree–No opinion

30. Police Action (Korea, Vietnam, but serving under non-U.S. officers)

Strongly disagree/ Disagree / Agree / Strongly Agree–No opinion

31. The United States runs a field training exercise. U.N. combat troops should be allowed to serve in U.S. combat units during these exercises under U.S. command and control.

Strongly disagree/ Disagree / Agree / Strongly Agree–No opinion

32. The United Nations runs a field training exercise. U.S. combat troops *under U.S. command* and control should serve in U.N. combat units during these exercises.

Strongly disagree/ Disagree / Agree / Strongly Agree–No opinion

33. The United Nations runs a field training exercise. U.S. combat troops should serve *under U.N. command* and control during these exercises.

Strongly disagree/ Disagree / Agree / Strongly Agree–No opinion

34. U.S. combat troops should participate in U.N. missions as long as the U.S. has full command and control.

Strongly disagree/ Disagree / Agree / Strongly Agree–No opinion

Exceptional Profile of Courage

35. U.S. combat troops should participate in U.N. missions under United Nations command and control.

Strongly disagree/ Disagree / Agree / Strongly Agree–No opinion

36. U.S. combat troops should be commanded by U.N. officers and non-commissioned officers (NCOs) at battalion and company levels while Performing U.N. missions.

Strongly disagree/ Disagree / Agree / Strongly Agree–No opinion

37. It would make no difference to me to have U.N. soldiers as members of my team. (e.g. fire team, squad, platoon)

Strongly disagree/ Disagree / Agree / Strongly Agree–No opinion

38. It would make no difference to me to take orders from a U.N. company commander.

Strongly disagree/ Disagree / Agree / Strongly Agree–No opinion

39. I feel the President of the United States has the authority to pass his responsibilities as Commander-in-Chief to the U.N. Secretary-General.

Strongly disagree/ Disagree / Agree / Strongly Agree–No opinion

40. I feel there is no conflict between my oath of office and serving as a U.N. soldier.

Strongly disagree/ Disagree / Agree / Strongly Agree–No opinion

41. I feel my unit's combat effectiveness would not be affected by performing humanitarian missions for the United Nations.

Strongly disagree/ Disagree / Agree / Strongly Agree–No opinion

42. I feel a designated unit of U.S. combat soldiers should be permanently assigned to the United Nations.

Strongly disagree/ Disagree / Agree / Strongly Agree–No opinion

43. I would be willing to volunteer for assignment to a U.S. combat unit under a U.N. commander.

Strongly disagree/ Disagree / Agree / Strongly Agree–No opinion

44. I would like U.N. member countries, including the U.S., to give the U.N. all the soldiers necessary to maintain world peace.

Strongly disagree/ Disagree / Agree / Strongly Agree–No opinion

45. I would swear to the following code:
"I am a United Nations fighting person. I serve in the forces which maintain world peace and every nation's way of life. I am prepared to give my life in their defense."

Strongly disagree/ Disagree / Agree / Strongly Agree–No opinion

46. The U.S. government declares a ban on the possession, sale, transportation, and transfer of all non-sporting firearms. A thirty (30) day amnesty period is permitted for these firearms to be turned over to the local authorities. At the end of this period, a number of citizen groups refuse to turn over their firearms. Consider the following statement:

I would fire upon U.S. citizens who refuse or resist confiscation of firearms banned by the U.S. government.

Strongly disagree/ Disagree / Agree / Strongly Agree–No opinion

In Section VII Conclusions, Page 84 of the document, it reads:
On September 26, 1994, President William Clinton speaking before the 49th Session of the U.N. General Assembly stated:

Exceptional Profile of Courage

"Our objectives should include ready, efficient and capable U.N. peacekeeping forces. And I am happy to report that, as I pledged to you last year, and thanks to the support in the United States Congress, $1.2 billion is now available from the United States for this critical account."

This study has dealt principally with two factors: The missions performed in operations other than war and transferring the *operational control authority* from U.S. to U.N.

Some in the U.S. Government are making the following argument:
"The United States cannot afford to engage in peacekeeping at the expense of combat readiness."

But the U.S. Congress can afford to pay the U.N. $1.2 billion to do so?

On Pages 58 and 59 of this same document, it states: The Department of Defense created a new office under the Secretary of Defense in May 1993. Sherri Wasserman Goodman was the first appointed Deputy under Secretary of Defense for Environmental Security. She controls several defense accounts whose multi-billion dollar assets are targeted for environmental projects. She stated:
"The Defense Department *environmental security* program was built in response to difficult challenges, including the transition to a new world order, a significantly downsized department and severe fiscal constraints."

Not only is the Department of Defense being tasked to participate in environmental missions, but apparently these missions will help transition to what they call "a new world order."

Chapter 2
"The American's Creed"
Accepted by the House of Representatives on behalf of all American citizens on April 3, 1918.

With so much social and political change taking place in our nation today, we need to know the fundamentals of our Constitution. In times of war as well as peace, it has provided us with a more enduring and practical government, and a greater degree of prosperity than any other nation ever.

The Constitution is important to the men and women in the Armed Services of the United States. For they have sworn an allegiance to the Constitution which is not formally required of private citizens. This oath is taken by all officers elected or appointed to civil or Armed Services:

"I do solemnly swear that I will support and defend the Constitution of the United States against all enemies, foreign and domestic; that I will bear true faith and allegiance to the same; that I take this obligation freely, without any mental reservation or purpose of evasion; and that I will well and faithfully discharge the duties of the office on which I am about to enter so help me God."

Even though private citizens are not required to take this oath, they are obligated by "The American's Creed" which was accepted by the House of Representatives on behalf of all American citizens on April 3, 1918.

Exceptional Profile of Courage

"I believe in the United States of America as a Government of the people, by the people, for the people; whose just powers are derived from the consent of the governed; a democracy in a republic; a sovereign Nation of many sovereign states; a perfect union, one and inseparable, established upon those principles of freedom, equality, justice and humanity for which American patriots sacrificed their lives and fortunes. I, therefore, believe it is my duty to my Country to love it; to support its Constitution; to obey its laws; to respect its flag; and to defend it against all enemies."

I believe is very important that we, as United States citizens, understand our duty to our Country. It is our obligation to teach our children to understand their duty to their Country. Let's take each duty of this creed:

I believe it is my duty to my Country to love it.

What is loving one's country mean? The Webster's dictionary tells us that love means a strong liking; fondness; good will. Being given this definition as a United States citizen, one must always look out for what is best for our Country; thereby, setting aside our personal desires that may harm the Constitution. Our desire should be to make sure the Country's safety and stability comes first. In doing so, we protect the rule of law which is the foundation of the United States Constitution. Each U.S. Citizen becomes a protector of the Constitution of the United States of America.

I believe it is my duty to my Country to support its Constitution.

Abraham Lincoln said, "Study the Constitution – Let every American, every lover of liberty, every well-wisher to his posterity swear by the blood of the Revolution never to violate in the least particular the laws of the country, and never to tolerate their violation by others. As the patriots of '76 did to the support of the

Declaration of Independence, so to the support of the Constitution and laws let every American pledge his life, his property, and his sacred honor. Let every man remember that to violate the law is to trample on the blood of his father, and to tear the charter of his own and his children's liberty ... Let it be taught in schools, in seminaries, and in colleges; let it be written in primers, in spelling books and in almanacs; let it be preached from the pulpit, proclaimed in legislative halls, and enforced in courts of justice...and, in short, let it become the political religion of the Nation, and, in particular, a reverence for the Constitution."

What is "supporting its Constitution?"

Getting involved in government, by voting, service, being knowledgeable of what is in the Constitution. Study the Constitution. Learning Constitutional Law, which is that part of public law that determines the political organization of a state, regulates the political relations between the state and the individuals who compose it.

I believe it is my duty to my Country to obey its laws.

We need to teach by example in obeying the laws set forth in the U.S. Constitution. In doing so, we teach our children to be good, law-abiding citizens which sets the next generation in good stead for obeying the law. We need to teach our children:

    1. Governments were instituted of God for the benefit of man; and that God will hold men and women accountable for their acts in relation to them, both in making laws and administering them, for the good and safety of society.

    2. No government can exist in peace, except such laws are framed and held inviolate as will secure to each individual the free exercise of conscience, the right and control of property, and the protection of life.

    3. All governments necessarily require civil officers and magistrates to enforce the laws of the same; and that such as will administer the law in equity and justice should be sought for and upheld by the voice of the people if a republic, or the will of the sovereign.

Exceptional Profile of Courage

It must be stated here that to know and assert one's legal rights is a duty of moral self-preservation, on the other hand, ignorance and neglect of those rights is moral suicide.

However, if the courts change your legal rights often, you may never know what your basic legal rights are. This action by the courts will disarm the individual and/or the public of their legal rights.

The Supreme Court of the United States was designed to uphold the law, not change it at their personal will.

> Precedent as a source of law should always predict the basis the Court uses for writing their decisions. No judge can use his or her own personal preference. For example, if the decision is based on their own theory, philosophy, set of personal values, ideas and opinions.

We the people care less what the judge personally thinks. We want the decisions based on precedent as the source law in writing the decision. The Constitution of the United States must be the rule of law. This great Nation becomes unstable if the law is changed by the courts on a daily basis. It's like a family that does not have a set of rules to abide by. Families that have fixed rules have greater success in keeping the family unit sound. There is enough precedent law to stabilize this Nation.

Let's remember that it is Congress that has the *legislative power*, not the executive branch or the judicial branch.

However, the expansion of the executive branch into the lawmaking business has developed gradually. Let's look at history:

> Since the Interstate Commerce Commission was developed in 1887, *various government agencies* have been issuing edicts known as "Administrative Law," which are enforceable in the courts just as much as the laws of Congress. Also, the Congress has passed broad enabling acts and delegated to the executive branch the power to issue "Executive Orders," which are endorsed as laws even though they are never officially approved by Congress, but are simply published in the "Federal Register." Today more laws are imposed on the

American people by these unconstitutional and irregular means than are passed by Congress. The idea of the President issuing executive orders as enforceable laws has gone through several stages.

Administrative Law

Body of law created by administrative agencies in the form of rules, regulations, orders, and decisions to carry out regulatory powers and duties of such agencies.

Executive Orders

An order or regulation issued by the President or some administrative authority under his directions for the purpose of interpreting, or giving administrative effect to a provision of the Constitution or of some law or treaty. To have the effect of law, such orders must be published in the Federal Registry.

The Constitutional Stage

In the beginning, the President or his cabinet officers issued executive orders to their *departments*. These were simply administrative orders and affected only the administrators and agencies of the government. In other words, they did not affect the public as the laws of Congress do.

Gradually, however, these executive orders began to increase in number and scope of influence. They began to affect the general public and not just the internal operations of government. Therefore, Executive Orders passed from the Constitution stage *to the strong President Stage*.

The transition to this new stage is indicated by the number of executive orders issued by the various Presidents. For example, President Cleveland issued only 71 executive orders; President McKinley issued merely 51 executive orders; President Theodore Roosevelt issued 1006 executive orders. President Clinton, in 1993, 1994 and 1995 issued 160. For years 1996–2000, I do not have the numbers yet.

From Theodore Roosevelt on, Presidents looked upon executive orders as a tool to demonstrate the power of the President to take independent action.

The World War I Stage

Under the urgency of the First World War, President Woodrow Wilson used the war powers to impose administrative law and executive orders on almost every phase of American life. For example, the Food Administration, the Grain Corporation, the War Trade Board, and the Committee on Public Information were all set up by executive orders without being specifically or individually authorized by Congress. On the basis of "implied authority" the President used his broad war powers to range across the entire economic and industrial horizon of America. The strict interpretation of Article I Section 1 of the U.S. Constitution has never been the same since.

The New Deal Stage

This covered both the Depression Era and the World War II years. Between them the use of executive orders became so broad that legislative powers emanating from the president and the executive branch became a permanent part of the lifestyle of America.

These executive orders became so numerous that in 1935 Congress passed the Federal Register Act. This act required the publication of all executive orders in the Federal Register and their subsequent filing with the U.S. Archives. The State Department previously had custody of these executive orders and began numbering all available orders in 1907.

It is estimated that the unnumbered orders lying in government files may be as many as 15,000 to 50,000. To gain some idea of the quantity of executive orders being poured out on the public as well as on government agencies, the official count by January 1985 had reached 12,498, according to Title 3 of the Code of Federal Regulation 1995 compilation.

Executive orders usually cite some authority for their issuance, but many of these would be totally irrational to the founders of this nation. In the early 1930s the Congress became nervous about delegating so much of its lawmaking power to the executive branch, and so it began monitoring the various agencies to make certain they were issuing executive orders in harmony with the original intent of Congress.

In 1984 the Supreme Court declared that it was a violation of the separation-of-powers doctrine to have the Congress monitoring the administration of the executive branch. Amazingly, the court did not say that it was a violation of the separation-of-powers doctrine to have the Congress delegating its lawmaking powers to the executive branch in the first place.

In addition to executive orders, there are *executive agreements*. Making *secret executive agreements* was never contemplated by the founders that the heads of nations would sit in a huddle and reach secret agreements other than temporary wartime strategies among allies.

To prevent the negotiation of secret agreement, the founders required that all treaties with foreign powers must be submitted to the Senate for approval.

During World War II the State Department began negotiating numerous secret arrangements as part of the allied war strategy, and this established a precedent for the so-called executive agreements which were accepted as commitments among the heads of state but were never presented to the Senate for ratification as treaties.

A typical example of an executive agreement was the Yalta Agreement which was worked out between President Franklin Delano Roosevelt, Winston Churchill, and Joseph Stalin in 1945. A statement was issued on February 11, 1945, but it soon became apparent that *other commitments were made* which were never presented to the Senate and were beyond the strategic agreements authorized by the War Power Act.

Under severe pressure, the State Department finally released the conference papers in March 1955, but held back certain sensitive material. To this day, neither the Senate nor the American public is completely aware of all the commitments made by FDR to the Soviet Union at Yalta.

Now, let's get back to the American Creed.

I believe it is my duty to my Country to respect its flag.

On June 4, 1777, a little less than a year after the Declaration of Independence, the Continental Congress adopted as the national flag of the United States a design of thirteen horizontal red and white stripes, with a union of thirteen white five-pointed stars on a blue field in the upper quarter next to the staff. The thirteen stripes and stars represented the thirteen states of the new nation, and the stars were usually arranged in a circle to symbolize the equality of the states.

After Vermont and Kentucky were admitted to the Union in 1791 and 1792, Congress passed an act in 1794 adding two more stripes and two more stars, so that for a number of years the flag had fifteen stripes and stars. This was the flag that Francis Scott Key saw flying over Fort McHenry in 1814, when he wrote "The Star Spangled Banner."

As the Nation continued to expand, it soon became obvious that adding a stripe for each new state would not be practical. In 1818 Congress passed an act which permanently set the number of stripes in the flag at thirteen – seven red and six white – and provided that a new star would be added for each new state.

By 1912 the number of states seemed complete with the admission of Arizona as the forty-eighth state and Congress ordered a forty-eight star flag designed with six horizontal and eight vertical rows of stars. This remained the official flag until the admission of Alaska and Hawaii, which added two more stars, making the total fifty.

What does the United States flag stand for?

We look upon our flag as the symbol of national union, freedom, and equality. The red of the flag stands for courage – the white for liberty – the blue for loyalty.

The thirteen stripes representing the thirteen colonies mean that in union there is strength. Each star represents an individual state, and the number of stars shows the growth of the nation. The flag is, therefore, not only a national emblem; it represents, also, the history of our nation. Its makers intended that the flag should tell this story to their children from generation to generation.

As citizens of the United States of America, we need to honor the flag. It should be important to all Americans to fly the flag from our homes on national holidays and other patriotic occasions.

When we Pledge Allegiance to the flag, it is not to any person or political party, but to the Constitution and the laws of the United States and to our ideals as American citizens.

When the flag is passing in a parade, or during the ceremony of raising or lowering or presenting and retiring the flag, all persons present should face the flag, stand at attention, and salute. Men should remove their hats with the right hand and hold it at the left shoulder, the hand being over the heart. Women should salute by placing the right hand over the heart. Aliens should stand at attention.

We all need to know the Pledge of Allegiance. "I pledge allegiance to the flag of the United States of America, and to the Republic for which it stands, one nation under God, indivisible, with liberty and justice for all."

Allegiance means loyalty. We as citizens of the United States of America must remember that this country was instituted of God for the benefit of those who live in this great country.

I believe it is my duty to my Country to defend it against all enemies.

We the citizens of the United States of America know that weakness and divisions at home will invite dangers from abroad, and that nothing would tend more to secure us from the enemy than union, strength and good government within ourselves.

Private passions of certain men and women lead to sacrifice of national tranquility. Men and women of this class, whether the

Exceptional Profile of Courage

favorites of a king or of a people, have in too many instances abused the confidence they possessed. They sacrifice the national tranquility to personal advantage or personal gratification.

Any attempt, whether from within or outside the United States, that cause disorder in the operation of the union or the break up of the union or the decay of the freedoms afforded by the U.S. Constitution to the citizens of the United States of America, is then an enemy to this Country and warrants the attention of each citizen.

The Second Amendment to the U.S. Constitution –

> "A well-regulated militia being necessary to the security of a free state, the right of the people to keep and bear arms shall not be infringed."

Recently, Federal and State courts have affirmed that the Second Amendment presents no bar against statutes requiring the *registration* of firearms, prohibiting the possession of submachine guns, and regulating the right to carry concealed weapons.

> These same courts have indicated the Second Amendment guarantees a collective not an individual right to bear arms. Note: President George W. Bush is restoring in 2002 the correct consitutional interpretation.

Most *state* Constitutions do give the individual the right to keep and bear arms such as the Utah Constitution states: Art I Sec. 6 (Right to Bear Arms) The individual right of the people to keep and bear arms for security and defense of self, family, others, property, or the state, as well as for other lawful purposes shall not be infringed; but nothing herein shall prevent the legislature from defining the lawful use of arms.

Many American citizens do not realize that they belong to the militia of their State. They confuse their State militia with the National Guard, which is a specialized reserve corps in each State *trained at federal expense* for immediate service.

Title 10, Section 31 of the U.S. Code: "The militia of each State includes all able-bodied males at least 17 years of age and under 45 years of age who are or have (made) a declaration of intent to become citizens."

The right to keep and bear arms, as described in the Second Amendment of the Constitution, was considered by the founders to be an unalienable right connected with the preservation of life, liberty and property. Today Americans are the best-armed civilian population in the World. The number of private citizens owning arms is estimated to be around fifty million (50,000,000). The number of firearms in the possession of private citizens is estimated to be between 150 and 200 million weapons.

It is a historical fact that in nations where the political leaders want to curtail the rights of the people and take away their property and freedom, they always begin by disarming them. This is usually done by first requiring them to register their firearms and imposing a heavy penalty on those who do not.

The clear intent of the Second Amendment may be found in the commentaries of those who wrote it and approved it as part of the Constitution. Here are some examples:

> Richard Henry Lee: "To preserve liberty it is essential that the whole body of the people always possess arms and be taught alike, especially when young, how to use them"
>
> Samuel Adams: "The said Constitution shall never be construed to authorize Congress to prevent the people of the United States who are peaceable citizens from keeping their own arms."
>
> Patrick Henry: "The great object is that every man be armed…Everyone who is able may have a gun."

These statements were taken from the carefully documented 1982 report by the Senate Subcommittee on the Constitution.

Chapter 3
Why a U.N.-Free Zone Ordinance

We must become knowledgeable of the past to enable us to understand the present and to be able to calculate with a clear mind the events of the future.

The last ten years, I've given a Constitutional Lecture Series on various subjects: Know Your Duty as a U.S. Citizen; Know Your Constitution as a U.S. Citizen; Know the Federalist Papers as a U.S. Citizen; What has Happened to the United States Constitution; Know the ACLU as a U.S. Citizen; Know the United Nations as a U.S. Citizen; and The Spirit of the Constitution.

A guest writer for the *Deseret News* in Salt Lake City has stated in one of his articles, "Too many Utahns are ignorant about the U.N." I agree with his statement. However, he suggests people do not know that the U.N. is a loving, peacekeeping, *feed the poor children of the world* organization. Is this true, or an over simplification.

As you read on, you will understand that there will be many local measures in our towns and states that the United Nations wants to institute. We must be prepared to handle these issues so we will be able to protect our Constitution, the Bill of Rights, our Republic type government, and most importantly the sovereignty of this great nation.

The United Nations is housed in New York City, between First Avenue and Roosevelt Drive and E. 42nd Street and E. 48th Street.

The list of their agencies is many: Food and Agriculture Organization FAO; International Atomic Energy Agency IAEA; International Bank for Reconstruction and Development IBRD (The World Bank); The International Development Association IDA; The International Finance Corporation IFC; Multilateral Investment Guarantee Agency MIGA; The International Center for Settlement of Investment Disputes ICSID; International Civil Aviation Organization ICAO; International Fund for Agricultural Development IFAD; International Labor Organization ILO; International Monetary Fund IMF; International Telecommunication Union ITU; United Nations Children's Fund UNICEF (this one may be familiar to you because the U.N. and news media promote);

> In fact, the United States of America has fed more people of this world than any other nation or organization including the U.N.

United Nations Educational, Scientific, and Cultural Organization UNESCO; United Nations High Commissioner for Refugees UNHCR; Universal Postal Union UPU (the U.N. has its own postal service); World Health Organization WHO; World Intellectual Property Organization WIPO; World Meteorological Organization WMO; World Trade Organization WTrO.

The U.N. is a fully organized government. It has over 52,200 people working within the U.N. System, which includes the Secretary General, General Assembly, Security Council, Economic and Social Council, Trusteeship Council, a budget over 2.53 billion dollars, and the International Court of Justice (World Court). These are only a few of the U.N. Organizations.

The U.N. is encouraging a one-world government tax. This international tax idea was originated by James Tobin, a Yale economist. In the 1970s he proposed a tax on international currency exchanges. Now some are looking at taxes or fees on carbon emissions, international internet activity, overseas e-mails, etc. Can a global income tax be far behind?

Exceptional Profile of Courage

The following material is used by permission of *The New American* magazine, October 22, 2001, Vol. 17, No. 22. "The Global Taxman." (Several Excerpts)

> "...In his original proposal, Tobin suggested the role of tax collector be played by either the IMF or the World Bank. Modern versions of the plan call for the creation of an entirely new tax collection bureaucracy...."

> "An astonishingly candid article by Kevin Baumert of the UN affiliate Global Policy Forum outlines the deceptive strategies used by proponents of global taxation:
> The process of implementing global levies will necessarily be slow and incremental. Thus it is important to take these small, incremental steps now, so that larger ones are possible in the future.... The first challenge is to get the tax implemented."

> "The very word 'tax' is loaded with negative connotations and is often synonymous with political death. For this reason, couching proposals in terms of a fee, levy, or charge will be decidedly more palatable to policymakers. A 'charge' or 'user fee' in fact makes more sense... of placing restrictions on the use of global commons (like air, sea, electronic frequencies, spaces in orbit, etc.)"

The United Nations planners of the One Child Policy feel there is a need to control what many see as a population explosion.

The following material is used by permission of *The New American* magazine, October 22, 2001, Vol. 17, No. 22. "UN Attack on World Population." (Several Excerpts)

> "...Maurice Strong, the Canadian socialist billionaire who served as the secretary-general of the U.N.'s Earth Summit (UNCED) in Rio de Janeiro deplored the world's 'explosive increase in population,' and warned, 'we have been the most successful species ever; we are now a

species out of control. 'Population,' he declared, 'must be stabilized, and rapidly.' "

"A 1994 report issued by the United Nation's Cairo Conference on Population and Development announced plans to regulate the most intimate of family matters: "The promotion of the *responsible* exercise of these rights [marriage and childbearing] for all people should be the fundamental basis for government- and community-supported policies and programmes in the area of reproductive health, including family planning." (Emphasis added)

"The same UN Cairo report states that 'reproductive health care in the context of primary health care should ... include ... abortion.'"

"According to Dr. Norman Myers, an advisor to the World Bank, the World Resources Institute, and various UN agencies, the populations of industrial nations such as Britain, Russia, and American should be reduced by one-half."

The U.N. believes it is important to disarm all citizens. The following material is used by permission of *The New American* magazine, October 22, 2001, Vol. 17, No. 22. "Civilian Disarmament." (Excerpts)

"UN Secretary-General Kofi Annan refers to privately owned firearms as 'weapons of mass destruction in slow motion'...The same claim is made in Our Global Neighborhood, the 1995 report of the UN-funded Commission on Global Governance (CGG). That report, which was created as a blueprint for UN reform, called for global measures to crack down on 'the rampant acquisition and use of increasingly lethal weapons by civilians – whether individuals seeking a means of self defense, street gangs, criminals, political opposition groups, or terrorist organizations.'"

Exceptional Profile of Courage

In the new book *Death by "Gun Control"* by Aaron Zelman and Richard W. Stevens, p3, the following statistics are provided:

In 1926, the Soviet Union established gun control. From 1929 to 1945, approximately 20 million dissidents, unable to protect themselves, were rounded-up and exterminated.

In 1911, Turkey established gun control. From 1915 to 1917, 1.5 million Armenians, unable to defend themselves, were rounded up and exterminated.

In 1938, Germany established gun control. From 1933 to 1945, 20 million Jews and others, unable to defend themselves, were rounded up and exterminated.

In 1914 and 1935, Nationalist China established gun control. From 1927 to 1949, 10 million political opponents and others, unable to defend themselves, were rounded up and exterminated.

In 1951 and 1957, China established gun control. From 1952 to 1976, 20 -35 million political dissidents, unable to defend themselves, were rounded up and exterminated.

In 1932, Guatemala established gun control. From 1960 to 1981, 100,000 to 200,000 Mayan Indians, unable to defend themselves, were rounded up and exterminated.

In 1970, Uganda established gun control. From 1971 to 1979, 300,000 Christians, unable to defend themselves, were rounded up and exterminated.

In 1938, Cambodia established gun control. From 1975 to 1979, two million educated people, unable to defend themselves, were rounded up and exterminated.

In 1979, Rwanda established gun control. In 1994, 800,000 Tutsi people, unable to defend themselves, were rounded up and exterminated.

From these statistics, we can see that in the 20th Century, because of gun control, 90 million or more defenseless people were rounded up and exterminated.

> George Washington warned:
> "When firearms go, it all goes!"

All good citizens are concerned about weapons being in the hands of criminals and terrorists. But is the answer really to take all the weapons of the good citizens, knowing the criminals and terrorists will always find the weapons they need?

The U.N. convention on Biological Diversity, which includes the Agenda 21, was formalized at the U.N. Earth Summit in 1992 as a master plan for sustaining societies. Agenda 21 will bind governments all over the world to the U.N. plan for changing the way we live, eat, learn, and communicate. Its regulations could severely limit our use of water, electricity, and transportation.

The following material is used by permission of *The New American* magazine, October 22, 2001, Vol. 17, No. 22. "The UN Attack on Property"

> "Across America property owners are under concerted attack. In the Klamath Basin of southern Oregon and northern California, hundreds of ranchers and farmers are being forced from the land by heavy-handed federal policies that have cut off their irrigation water, ostensibly for the benefit of sucker fish that have been declared 'endangered.'....
>
> "What many of these besieged citizens are beginning to realize is that there is a connection between the outrages they are experiencing and the United Nations... to be proceeding from various UN environmental treaties and conventions.
>
> "A number of frightful programs emerged from the UN's 1992 Earth Summit in Rio de Janeiro. One of them is the Convention on Biological Diversity, supposedly crafted to protect our planet's ... ecosystems. It is accompanied by a huge 1,140 page instrument known as the Global Biodiversity Assessment (GBA)...In 1993, President Clinton began implementing the GBA, even though the United States had not ratified the treaty."

It has become a very local issue for Americans when the U.N.

tells them to move off their land because its been designated as a biosphere, which means off-limits to humans. And around this biosphere will be a *buffer* zone.

> Remember, there are 47 or more Biosphere Reserves and 20 or more World Heritage sites occupying 50 million acres of United States soil controlled by the U.N. (See Biosphere Reserved & World Heritage Sites list)

Water is also a local issue. The United Nations at its Earth Summit in Rio 1992, adopted Agenda 21, which calls for freshwater protection. It calls for the regulation on the amount of water withdrawn annually from both groundwater and surface water sources.

For agriculture and other uses, Agenda 21 states that water withdrawals "must be limited to a percentage of total annual flow." Agenda 21 also sets a percentage of water of withdrawal as an indicator of the health of biodiversity, which means the lower the percentage of water withdrawn, the healthier its biodiversity.

Nine reasons why my City Council in LaVerkin, Utah, passed an ordinance in regard to the United Nations:

1. Because authority to govern in this country is derived from The People, not from the national government. Power flows upward, not down.

2. Because the City Council members took an oath to support and defend the Constitution of the United States of America.

3. Because my city, my county, and my state are losing their constitutional protections to the United Nations, and Washington is not acting to protect them.

4. Because it is incumbent upon the City Council to educate the citizenry. Each City Council member is a leader. The Ordinance makes a statement that shapes the public debate, and educates The People.

5. Because the City Council will be assisting in a growing groundswell of public opinion that is becoming more and more aware of the goals of the United Nations.

6. Because the United Nations is looking hard at the concept of Private Property.

7. Because radical environmentalists are attacking our authority on every side, attempting to reduce our control over our private property, and are using United Nations rulings to do so. They come in uniforms of Park Rangers, Dept. of Energy, environmentalists sampling the water, the soil, the air. They come with restrictions on what we can and cannot grow, where we can and cannot dump fill dirt, or excavate. They tell us where roads can and cannot be.

8. Because the courts have consistently recognized the authority of local governments to make resolutions and local ordinances affecting national policy, because it is our birthright.

9. By the authority invested in the City Council, the encroachment on our individual and local rights can be interrupted, and we can start taking back our country, one town and one county at a time by passing an U.N.–Free Zone Ordinance.

It's important that Americans learn the guarantees of the U.S. Constitution. By doing so, we will have a better understanding why we need to protect and preserve it. The Preamble gives us an overview of its intent:

We the People of the United States, in order to form a more perfect Union, establish Justice, insure domestic Tranquility, provide for the common defense, promote the general Welfare, and secure the Blessings of Liberty to ourselves and our Posterity, do ordain and establish this Constitution for the United States of America.

Let's take each part of the Preamble.

We the People of the United States

Take note that this is a government of the *people*, not of the States. Following the Articles of Confederation, the Constitution brought forth a new Nation, deriving its just powers from the *consent of the governed.*

> **"The people,** the highest authority known to our system from whom all our institutions spring and on whom

Exceptional Profile of Courage

they depend, formed it," said President Monroe.

Patrick Henry exclaimed, "**We the People** is the institution of one great consolidated National government of the people of all the States, instead of a government by compact with the States for its agents."

In Order to form a more perfect Union

Meaning *a more perfect Union* than had been achieved by the Articles of Confederation. Washington, in his Farewell Address states, "a government for the whole is indispensable.... The Union, made *more perfect* by the Constitution."

Establish Justice, insure domestic Tranquility, provide for the common defense

Establish Justice is one principle that this great nation is founded on – the administration of law. The Constitution is the rule of law and every citizen is held to its standard. No one is above the law.

Insure domestic tranquility means our country would have a serene prevailing mood where all the citizens could live in harmony.

Provide for the common defense means that all citizens would be protected from harm by any and all enemies of this nation.

Therefore, we have national unity, justice, peace at home, liberty, and security for all citizens of this great nation.

Promote the general Welfare, and secure the Blessings of Liberty to ourselves and our Posterity, do ordain and establish this Constitution for the United States of America.

In the Declaration of Independence *firm reliance on the protection of Divine Providence* is expressed, and in the Articles of Confederation it is mentioned that "it has pleased the Great Governor of the world to incline the hearts of the legislatures we respectively represent in Congress to approve of and to authorize us to ratify the said Articles of Confederation and perpetual Union."

In a Supreme Court action (1892) involving a minister of the gospel from England (Alien Contract Labor Law) coming to America to accept service in a New York church –

In applying the rule of statutory interpretation, that the exact meaning of the legislature must be adhered to, the court said, *"no purpose of action against religion could be imputed to any legislation"* when the language did not clearly express it, for the reason that the commission given by Ferdinand and Isabella to Columbus down through all the charters to the colonies, as well as in the Declaration of Independence and in all the State Constitutions, there is to be found "a *profound reverence for religion and an assumption that its influence in all human affairs is essential to the well-being of the United States.*"

One who reads closely the full meaning of each statement, clause or word in the Constitution will find that it was carefully written to protect the individual – his life, liberty and property.

The Constitution was fashioned for the protection against the abuse of power by his servants in the legislature, whom he may dismiss by ballot or by impeachment, and against invasion of his rights by an appeal to the courts; against his state or federal officers, whom he may dismiss by ballot or by impeachment; against his judges, whom he may remove for lack of *good behavior*. His government is his servant not his master, as the King has always been.

In questions of power, wrote Jefferson, "Let no more be heard of confidence in man, but bind him down from mischief by the chains of the Constitution."

The founding fathers of the Constitution feared abuse of power by political parties as much as they did abuses by Kings. "Wherever there is an interest and power to do wrong, wrong will generally be done, and not less readily by a powerful and interested party than by a powerful and interested prince," wrote James Madison to Thomas Jefferson in 1788.

> "The only thing necessary for evil to triumph is
> for good men to do nothing."
> Edmund Burke 1729-1797

Chapter 4
Evaluation of the Ordinance by Herbert W. Titus, a Legal Advisor to Congressman Paul (R-Texas).

The LaVerkin City Council and the Citizens of LaVerkin received a letter from Herbert W. Titus, who is a legal advisor to Congressman Paul's "The Liberty Committee," which Dr. Paul founded and of which Dr. Paul is honorary chairman. Mr. Titus' research and thinking are reflected in HR 1146.

See the web site: thelibertycommittee.org

To: The LaVerkin, Utah City Council
and the Citizens of LaVerkin, Utah
From: Herbert W. Titus
Subject: The LaVerkin Un-free Zone Ordinance Is Constitutional
Date: July 24, 2001

On July 24, 2001, as Pioneer Day is celebrated across the state of Utah, the people of LaVerkin, Utah, and their elected representatives on the City Council, are defending their pioneering effort to restore American independence and sovereignty through the enactment, on July 4, 2001, of their United Nations-Free Zone Ordinance.

As was true of the pioneers who came before them 154 years ago, the LaVerkin pioneers are being attacked for not being politically correct. To aid this attack, the ACLU and others have marshaled their forces claiming that the UN-Free Zone ordinance is unconstitutional. This claim is not true.

Al Snow, Sr.

At the heart of the LaVerkin UN-Free zone ordinance is the city council's finding that the United Nations is a wholly illegitimate and unconstitutional organization. This finding, in turn, is based upon the incontrovertible fact that the United Nations Charter is not a treaty, but a Constitution for a world government.

Just as the Preamble of the United States Constitution states "We the People of the United States," the Preamble to the United Nations Charter states "We the Peoples of the United Nations."

Just as Article V of the United States Constitution provides for binding amendments without unanimous approval of the fifty States, so Article 108 of the United Nations Charter provides for binding amendments without the unanimous approval of its member states.

Just as Article IV, Section 3 authorizes Congress to admit additional States into the Union without obtaining the consent of the States, so Article 4, Section 2 empowers the General Assembly of the United Nations to admit additional nations without obtaining consent of the member nations.

And just as Article VI of the United States Constitution provides that it is the Supreme Law of the Land, Article 103 of the United Nations Charter provides that the Charter prevails over any and all other international agreements.

According to the laws of nature and of nature's God, as recited in America's Declaration of Independence, and Article VI of the United States Constitution, only the people, acting through their elected representatives in constitutional convention, have the power to ratify governing charters such as the United States Constitution and the United Nations Charter.

While the United States Constitution was submitted to the people for ratification, and so ratified, the United Nations Charter has never been submitted to the American people for ratification, but only to the United States Senate.

Exceptional Profile of Courage

The Senate, however, has no authority to adopt such an all-encompassing governing charter, especially one that authorizes that charter's officials, as do Articles 104 and 105 of the United Nations Charter, to enter the geographic territories of member nations to carry out their responsibilities enjoying all the privileges and immunities of civil government officials.

Having never been properly ratified as a new constitution for the American people, the United Nations Charter is not legally binding, as the law of the land. To the contrary, the Charter, and the United Nations General Assembly, Security Council, and all other bodies created by that Charter, are illegitimate, and contrary to the Constitution of the United States.

According to Article VI of the United States Constitution, and to their oaths of office, the LaVerkin City Council has the duty to support the Constitution of the United States, not the United Nations Charter.

Pursuant to that duty and their oaths of office, the City Council enacted its UN Free-Zone ordinance. That ordinance, in turn, is designed to protect the sovereignty of the city and its people from any and all unconstitutional UN operations within the city limits.

To that end, Section 3.E. of the ordinance prohibits United Nations officials and its officially funded programs from operating in the city.

Section 4 prohibits the official display of the United Nations flag and any effort of the United Nations to exercise civil or criminal jurisdiction within the city limits.

Section 5 prohibits the city from doing business with the United Nations or its affiliates.

Section 6 requires persons within the city limits to notify the public that they do business with the United Nations. Violation of these prohibition is a Class C misdemeanor.

The ACLU and others would have the people of LaVerkin believe that such prohibitions are unconstitutional violations of the United Nations personnel's rights of freedom of speech and association. But no United Nations personnel has any lawful authority on LaVerkin soil.

The LaVerkin ordinance does not, however, prohibit any such person from speaking out on behalf of the United Nations or even associating for the purpose of promoting UN activities. What it does prohibit is any official city affiliation or cooperation with the UN, or any private commercial relationships with the U.N. without proper notice to the public.

Finally, some would have the people of LaVerkin believe that their City Council has no authority to act to protect their residents from the unconstitutional and illegal acts of the United Nations. They claim that the President and the Congress has "preempted" the city council because the United Nations is a matter of foreign affairs not domestic concern.

But the constitutional duty of the LaVerkin City Council under Article VI of the United States Constitution cannot be preempted; nor can it be maintained that the unconstitutional United Nations is not operating domestically in matters of local concern.

The LaVerkin United Nation-Free Zone Ordinance is, therefore, constitutional.

Chapter 5
Pertinent Facts About the United Nations

The United Nations Charter, signed June 26, 1945, created the United Nations on October 24, 1945, after the Charter had been ratified by the five permanent members of the Security Council – China, France, the USSR, the United Kingdom and the United States.

To understand how the United Nations came to be, one must understand the historic events that led to its formation.

During World War II, as a result of the aggression of Germany against the United States and communist Soviet Union, the two countries had become uneasy but necessary allies. The negotiated peace pact to end the war required ongoing Soviet participation with the Allies, even though significant ideological differences existed.

> Communism, a system of government in which the state plans and controls the economy and a single, authoritarian party holds power, was portrayed as a higher social order that benefited the common man, with all goods shared equally by the people so governed.

The United States, prior to World War II, had gone through difficult years of the Great Depression and secret groups of Americans believing communism was the solution, began to work toward that end. They had to work underground because bringing communism to their country meant overthrowing the present government. Communist sympathizers were found in all walks of life in the United States, including the government.

Two weeks after Pearl Harbor occurred, which thrust America into World War II, members of a Foreign Policy Committee, under the direction of Secretary of State Cordell Hull, began looking for ways and means to establish international peace and security. All but one of the members of this committee were also members of the Council on Foreign Relations.

> The CFR, a private organization of 2000 or more members of international bankers, politicians, industrialists, militarists, economists, educators and media executives with affiliated bodies in England, Belgium, Denmark, India, France, Italy, Greece and Turkey, was dedicated to the establishment of a world system of government.

Enlarging on the earlier plan of the League of Nations, the Foreign Policy Committee worked throughout WW II to form what they would call the United Nations.

When the U.N. Organizing Conference was held in San Francisco in 1945 following the end of the war, 47 members of the CFR were among the American delegation.

With the exception of Dean Acheson, a number of State Department and Treasury Department officials who helped to shape the U.N. Charter were later identified in sworn testimony as secret communist agents, including Alger Hiss..

Alger Hiss was one of the two chief architects of the U.N. Charter. He also presided over the San Francisco organizing conference.

Leo Pasvolsky (CFR), born of Russian Revolutionary parents, joined our State Department in 1934 and rose rapidly to a position that enabled him to virtually write the final draft of the U.N. Charter, which appeared to be patterned after the Soviet Constitution.

Exceptional Profile of Courage

It was Pasvolsky who explained the Charter's contents to members of the United States Senate before it voted U.S. membership in the U.N.

> The only two Senators who actually read the Charter in its entirety before they voted were the only two to vote against U.S. membership in the United Nations. They were Senators William Langer of North Dakota and Henrik Shipstead of Minnesota.

President Roosevelt, Alger Hiss, Charles Boden, and Joseph Stalin had agreed at a Yalta conference in 1945 that the Soviets would receive votes for the U.S.S.R., Byelorussia, and the Ukraine. So the Soviet Union had (and still has) three votes in the U.N. General Assembly to only one for the United States and other member nations.

A Soviet (Russian) national has always held the position of Under Secretary General for Political and Security Council Affairs – a position which holds ultimate authority over and control of all U.N. military, nuclear and disarmament operations.

Trygve Lie, Secretary General of the U.N. (1946-1952), revealed in his book, *In The Cause of Peace*, that the Soviet Union insisted that the U.N. headquarters be located on U.S. soil.

How Has World Peace Succeeded Under the U.N.

Since the U.N. was created, over 800 million people have come under Communist rule. Communist governments violated to every extreme the U.N. Declaration of human rights by murdering and imprisoning millions of their citizens.

Despite a U.N. Resolution not to intervene in an internal conflict between Katanga's Christian, anti-communist president, Moise Tshombe, and the communist-controlled Congolese government under Patrice Lumumba, U.N. forces were ordered to invade Katanga to compel its subjugation to Leopoldville.

Al Snow, Sr.

It is interesting to note that U.N. Military non-intervention seemed to occur when causes of violence were communist-inspired and backed. For example –

The ineffective action of the U.N. in East Germany, Cuba, Hungary, Poland, Latvia, Estonia, Lithuania, Vietnam, Angola, Tibet, Malaysia and the Dominican Republic. In some cases the causes of violence were communist-inspired and backed, as in Cuba and Tibet; or they were the actions of an oppressed people attempting to break the chains of a communist slave state, as in East Germany and Hungary.

The Korean and Vietnam Wars were United Nations managed operations.

In Vietnam, the chain of command lead from the U.N. Security Council, then headed by Leonid Kutakov (a Soviet communist), through the Southeast Asia Collective Defense Treaty – (SEATO being a "Regional Arrangement" of the U.N., with headquarters in Bangkok, Thailand) – to Lt. General Creighton W. Abramns, whose predecessor was Gen. William Westmoreland.

Many U.S. veterans of these wars are angry at the loss of American lives, believing that the strategies of the U.N. seemed not to focus on winning the war, but in *managing* the war.

Transfer of U.S. Military Power to the U.N.

The authority to transfer the United States military to the United Nations central control was solidified by Congress in 1961 via Public Law 87-297, the "Arms Control and Disarmament Act" (H.S. 9118, 87th Congress, Sept. 26, 1961).

State Department Document 7277 – Freedom From War: The United States Program for General and Complete Disarmament in a Peaceful World details a three-stage plan to disarm all nations and arm the U.N. Under the final stage, "no state would have the military power to challenge the progressively strengthened U.N. Peace Force."

Under Chapters IX and X of the U.N. Charter, the U.N. is given the authority to enforce domestic policy dealing with equal employment, human rights, economic development, cultural matters and matters relating to health. It is under these sections of the Charter that many specialized agencies have been set up, and their policies dealing with many domestic matters have been enacted into law in the United States, *after first having been pronounced by the agencies of the United Nations.*

Chapter XVI of the U.N. Charter, including Articles 102-105, gives the U.N. the right to "physically come onto or occupy the land territory of a member state, for fulfillment of its purposes."

The International Covenant on Civil and Political Rights was adopted by the U.S. Senate in April, 1992. The intent of this legislation is to circumvent the Connally Amendment (which was proposed specifically to prevent the U.N. from interfering in United States internal affairs).

> Now, the U.N. and World Court can intervene in individual rights and liberties and local government, according to former Congressman John R. Rarick, who authored legislation to get the United States out of the U.N.

As evidenced by the General Assembly vote to seat Red China and oust the Nationalist Chinese Government on Formosa, the United States and other so-called "free nations" can be greatly out-voted on most any issue by a combination of the (former) communist bloc nations and the African Asian bloc countries.

> The Council of Global Government, which met at the U.N. in New York City in 2001, to amend the United Nations Charter, proposes to eliminate veto power and permanent membership status on the Security Council. Our one vote means little.

The federal government did not have the constitutional authority to ratify the United Nations Charter (Treaty), because powers of government are reserved to the states and to the people by the Constitution.

> In the 1950s an Amendment was introduced into the Senate, sponsored by Senator John Bricker of Ohio, called the Bricker Amendment. It stated that any provision of a treaty that conflicted with the Constitution, that the Constitution would be the Supreme Law of the Land. Being an Amendment it required a two-thirds vote for passage. Sixty Senators voted for it and thirty one against, losing by just one vote

The States, as original parties to the Constitutional compact, have both the legal right and the duty to challenge this usurpation of power and actions by federal agents.

The United States Congress, which passed the U.N. Participation Act, also has the power and authority to terminate U.S. membership in the U.N.

Under Section 3 (a) of P.L. 87-297, "armaments of all kinds" are to be reduced or eliminated. This could be construed by a federal court or the World Court to include the personal arms of private citizens, which are presently protected by the Second Amendment to the Constitution.

By voting for the United Nations General Agreement on Tariffs and Trade, Congress surrendered a major element of its Constitutional Power to "lay and collect taxes, duties, imposts and excises."

> Now the World Trade Organization (WTO) – an international agency in which the United States has but one vote of 123 – will call the shots on American trade policies.

Only our elected officials at the national and state levels of government can restore the rights guaranteed by the Constitution.

Exceptional Profile of Courage

One might ask: Do they really know the issues we have discussed herein?

Or, have they, like many Americans, depended on the media for an interpretation of critical issues.

J. Ruben Clark, Jr., former Under-Secretary of State and Ambassador to Mexico, who was widely recognized as one of our nation's foremost international lawyers, stated on page 27 of the book *The United Nations Today*:

> "Not only does the Charter Organization (United Nations) not prevent future wars, but it makes it practically certain that we shall have future wars, and as to such wars it takes from us (the United States) the power to declare them, to choose the side on which we shall fight, to determine what forces and military equipment we shall use in war, and to control and command our sons who do the fighting."

Chapter 6
U.N. Declared a Sovereign World Government, 1970

The United Nations was given full diplomatic recognition as a Sovereign World Government on March 19, 1970.

> Historians of the future may point to this date as the day the United States of America became an arm of a one-world government.

This action gave the moribund United Nations astounding new life by the new U.S. Senate action, paving the way for a cadre of new United Nations proposals including a World Tax; the push to ratify the Genocide Treaty, and the United Nations obtaining valuable space for a new $300 million U.N. building in New York City.

Passage happened quietly, unnoticed by the news media, in a Senate chamber only partly filled. In this almost sleepy atmosphere, with the Senators going on and on endlessly, the Presiding Officer suddenly refused to recognize another Senator and addressed the Senate floor himself.

"The Senate will proceed to vote" he said, "on Executive J, first session, 91st Congress, the Convention on the Privileges and Immunities of the United Nations. The question is: Will the Senate advise and consent to the resolution of ratification? On this question, the yeas and nays have been ordered, and the clerk will call the roll."

The count at the end of the vote – 78 yeas and 0 nays, with 22 Senators absent.

> From this moment on the United Nations would no longer be known as a mere "International Organization." Now the United Nations would have the status of full diplomatic recognition as a Sovereign Government.

This action had its full dress rehearsal the day before, when majority leader Mike Mansfield gained the floor, at a time *when no quorum was present*, and said the following:

> "Mr. President, discussion of this convention should not long detain the Senate. As a matter of fact, the Senate has already once approved it in 1947, by passing a joint resolution authorizing the President to accept it on behalf of the United States, but for essentially irrelevant reasons the joint resolution did not pass the House. Now some 20 years later, the matter is back for approval IN THE FORM OF A TREATY.
>
> "During this time, the provisions of the International Organization Immunities Act of 1945 and of the Headquarters Agreement Act of 1947 have provided the necessary privileges and immunities for most of the officers covered by the convention. Apparently the executive branch was satisfied with this situation, but THE UNITED NATIONS WAS NOT. One hundred and one of its members have become parties to the convention, but the United States, the principle host government, did not.
>
> "The anomaly of this situation has not escaped other United Nations members, as a reflection of the last of U.S. interest in the United Nations.
>
> "Briefly, the convention provides for certain immunities and privileges to the United Nations as an organization, to the representatives of member states, to United Nations officials and to experts on missions for the United Nations.
>
> "While the convention largely (to be voted on) represents the existing practice in regard to immunities and privileges, *it does enlarge upon them.*

"Since the Senate's advise and consent of the United Nations enabling act of 1945, the Immunities Act, 1945, and the Headquarters Agreement Act, 1947, the United Nations has looked upon itself as a sort of World Government *de facto*. Now it has become a World Government *de jure*."

You need to be familiar with these phrases.

De facto means – in fact, in deed, actually. This phrase is used to characterize an officer, a government, a past action, or a state of affairs which must be accepted for all practical purposes, but is illegal or illegitimate.

De jure means – descriptive of a condition in which there has been total compliance with all requirements of law. Therefore, a de facto government is one serving and functioning as a government, but one not permanently established and recognized as such. A de jure government is a legally established and lawfully recognized government.

In 1970 President Richard Nixon, giving the United Nations another shot in its ailing arm, called upon schools and colleges all over the nation to hold an annual United Nations day, *when they conduct model United Nations sessions.*

Since we are talking about United Nations Day, which is on October 24 each year, let's talk about United States Day on October 23 each year. The United States Day Committee founded "United States Day" on October 23, 1953. In 2001 we celebrated its 48th anniversary.

October 23 is a day for every American to reflect on the things that make America the greatest nation in the world – our divinely inspired Constitution, with its Bill of Rights (individual human rights) and a free enterprise economic system that has made our prosperity the envy of every nation on earth. Our system of government and the blessing flowing therefrom should make us the leader and example of the world.

On April 25, 1970, twelve high schools took part in conducting United Nations sessions at Chapman College located in California.

In 1970 the United Nations also pushed for "World Habeas Corpus," according to the March 26, 1970 Congressional Record, in an article by Rep. Pucinski of Illinois. Pucinski suggested that we needed a World Habeas Corpus System, in order to "protect human rights; in every nation according to the United Nations Declaration of Human Rights."

> Habeas Corpus is a writ to test or challenge the legality of the restraints or holds on a person's liberty. The traditional purpose of the writ is to secure the release of a defendant from illegal incarceration or illegal restraint of any kind.

World Habeas Corpus, ipso facto, is just one more step closer to World Government. It must be remembered that only governments can grant habeas corpus, so we must assume that in 1970 the United Nations considered itself a World Government

Al Snow, Sr.

Chapter 7
It All Began with the League of Nations
Events 1916 thru 1935

The League of Nations, a world organization established January 10, 1920, to promote international cooperation and peace, was first proposed by President Woodrow Wilson. But the United States never joined the League due to the objections of Congress, who felt it was designed as a one-world government. Essentially powerless, the League of Nations was officially dissolved in 1946. The League of Nations concept eventually led to creation of the United Nations.

These ideas began between 1815 and 1920 with a steady stream of literature advocating a united world of peace and prosperity. Then came World War I.

Why a League of Nations
On May 27, 1916, President Wilson called for the creation of a League of Nations before the group "League to Enforce Peace," to keep peace in the world once World War I in Europe had ended.

President Wilson maintained that the rule by force should end and that the United States would be willing to join in an organization that would ensure the freedom of the seas, protect all small countries from aggression and stop wars which had begun in violation of treaties. President Wilson said the world has a right to live in peace.

Woodrow Wilson in a speech to Americans:

Exceptional Profile of Courage

". . . There has been no greater advance than this, gentlemen. If you look back upon the history of the world you will see how helpless peoples have too often been a prey to powers that had no conscience in the matter. It has been one of the many distressing revelations of recent years that the great power which has just been, happily, defeated put intolerable burdens and injustices upon the helpless people of some of the colonies which it annexed to itself; that its interest was rather their extermination than their development; that the desire was to possess their land for European purposes, and not to enjoy their confidence in order that mankind might be lifted in these places to the next higher level.

"Now, the world, expressing its conscience in law, says there is an end of that, that our consciences shall be settled to this thing. States will be picked out which have already shown that they can exercise a conscience in this matter, and under their tutelage the helpless peoples of the world will come into a new light and into a new hope."

Source: 65 Congress, 3 Session, Senate Document No. 389, pp. 12-15

January 25, 1919, in Paris the League of Nations plan was adopted by Allies.

January 27, 1919, despite reservations, 19 small nations approved the League of Nations plan.

April 8, 1919, Geneva was named as the League of Nations headquarters.

May 30, 1919, President Wilson speaking at a Memorial Day ceremony stated that the League of Nations was a mandate of our dead.

November 19, 1919, the U.S. Senate voted against the Versailles Treaty, designed to end the war in Europe. (See Definitions). Republicans in Congress saw the League of Nations as a world government.

January 10, 1920, the Treaty of Versailles went into effect, but the United States tells Germany they are still at war.

January 16, 1920, in Paris the League of Nations holds its first meeting.

February 19, 1920, the United States Senate denies ratification of the Versailles Treaty.

March 15, 1920, by a 7 vote margin, the United States Senate, for the second time, refused to ratify the Treaty of Versailles, ending a long bitter fight. At the insistence of a majority of Democrats, the Senate made a renewed effort to approve the Treaty after it was rejected by a large margin on November 19, 1919. In an attempt to reverse the earlier votes, a compromise plan had been worked out by a group of Republican and Democratic Senators.

March 23, 1920, Britain denounces the United States for delay in joining the League of Nations.

May 16, 1920, Switzerland joins the League of Nations.

September 5, 1920, in Marion, Ohio, President Harding promises if elected *to seek revision* of the Versailles Treaty so the United States could join the League of Nations.

November 11, 1920, in Brownsville, Texas, President-elect Harding in his speech declares the United States fought war to protect American rights, not to make the *world* safe for democracy.

November 15, 1920, Nations raise flags in Geneva; the League of Nations opens first regular session.

December 8, 1920, President Wilson declines to send representative to the League of Nations meeting in Geneva.

December 15, 1920, in Geneva, China wins place on the League of Nations council; also admits Austria.

Exceptional Profile of Courage

April 12, 1921, President Warren Harding told a joint session of Congress that the United States "will have no part in the League of Nations." The new President's rejection of the League of Nations, which his Democratic predecessor, Woodrow Wilson, had labored so hard to fashion, drew loud cheers, primarily from his fellow Republicans. While rejecting the League of Nations, the new President promised his administration would *cooperate* with foreign governments in forming what he termed *a non-political association* of Nations and in rehabilitating war-torn European nations.

July 2, 1921, in Raritan, N.J., President Harding signed the peace decree ending war with Germany.

August 25, 1921, Germany signs peace treaty with United States officially ending state of war.

February 15, 1922, in Holland, the World Court opens at the Hague.

March 3, 1923, the United States Senate rejects entry into the World Court vote 49 to 24.

June 21, 1923, President Harding lauds the World Court to St. Louis audience but supports U.S. separation from the League of Nations.

January 27, 1926, the United States Senate votes to join the World Court with five reservations. (see Definitions).

September 2, 1926, in Geneva, Canada bars the United States entry into the World Court, saying the fifth reservation gives the United States virtual veto. In this case, the 5th reservation allowed the United States a veto power, which Canada did not like, since Canada didn't have a veto power.

February 9, 1927, the United States drops World Court hopes as British reject terms of admission.

Al Snow, Sr.

December 11, 1927, 395 world leaders sign a letter to President Coolidge asking United States to join the World Court.

December 9, 1929, the United States envoy in Geneva signs "Root Formula" (the basic plan) calling for United States to join the World Court.

September 4, 1930, in Geneva, Frank Kellogg, an American lawyer and diplomat who formerly served in the United States Senate and was Ambassador to Great Britain in 1924, accepts election to the World Court despite official non-participation of the United States.

January 29, 1935, the United States again votes down entry to the International Court of Justice.

Note: Even during the 1920s and 1930s, many people in the U.S. were concerned about protecting their constitutional rights. They could see how a political relationship could slowly encroach on American liberty.

Chapter 8
Birth of the United Nations

The world earnestly hoped that World War I would be the last war. Then came Hitler and World War II.

The nations of the world felt they must enact an organization to maintain world peace. Proposals to establish such an organization led to convening of the United Nations Conference on International Organization at San Francisco, California on April 25 through June 26, 1945, whereby the Charter of the United Nations was drawn up.

The Charter was signed on June 26 by 50 nations, and by Poland, one of the original 51 members of the United Nations, on October 15, 1945. The Charter came into effect on October 24, 1945, upon ratification by the permanent members of the Security Council and a majority of other signatures.

This United Nations, as of 1945, was to become a *pattern for world government.*

Events Leading To The Signing of United Nations Charter

At the San Francisco Convention, much ground work had been laid by various groups in the United States and elsewhere. It needed to be designed to make sure the world organization would be acceptable to the United States, which had rejected membership in the League of Nations after World War I.

Approximately three years had passed before the actual formation of the United Nations (which replaced the League of Nations). During this time various people and organizations in the U.S. conducted a full blown, expensive campaign to overcome the objections of those who were concerned they would have to give up their national sovereignty.

The International Free World Association was organized in 1941 and this organization started publishing a magazine, *Free World*. Secretary of the group, Louis Daliver, was identified later as a member of the Communist Party, see IPR Hearings, 1951 – 51 p. 526.

> The very fact the United Nations was envisioned from the very start by its planners as a world government, superseding the sovereignty of nations, was never hid from the public. On August 6, 1946, the *Chicago Tribune* published a news article stating the plans for a one-world government by the United Nations. The heading was this, "Radicals, Rich United to Push World State."

The United States State Department and the private organization Council on Foreign Relations played a very important role in conditioning the United States Congress and the general public to accept the United Nations and its restrictions on United States national sovereignty. (See State Department publication 3580 (1950) p. 108.)

> This sub-committee on International Organization was headed by Summer Wells of the State Department. Two members of this sub-committee had also served on the staff of Col. E. M. House at the Paris Peace Conference in 1918. They were Dr. James T. Shotwell and Isaiah Bowman.

A conference in Moscow was attended by top officials from the United States, Russia, Great Britain, and China long before the San Francisco Conference. The conference in Moscow was held under the watchful eye of Joseph Stalin and received his approval.

Final plans for the United Nations were planned by a top United States official, Alger Hiss, who was later exposed as a Soviet spy working inside the United States government.

Exceptional Profile of Courage

To understand fully the planning behind the United Nations prior to 1945, we need to look more closely at the "Free World Association," which had close ties to the United States State Department.

The objectives of the Free World Organization were spelled out as early as October 1942 in *Free World* –

"The creation of the machinery for a world government in which the United Nations will serve as a nucleus is a necessary task of the present in order to prepare in time the foundations for a future world order."

The United Nations Moves Forward

After the founding of the United Nations in 1945, various organizations organized around the support and defense of the U.N.

The earliest organization was United World Federalists, founded on February 22, 1947. It was made up of several other organizations that were interested in a one-world government: Americans United for World Government; World Federalists; World Republic; World Citizens of Georgia; Massachusetts Committee for World Federation and Student Federalists. (*New York Times* February 23, 1947 page 25.)

Their idea for a one-world government is stated in their quote:
"...world peace can be created and maintained only under world law, universal and strong enough to prevent armed conflict between nations. Therefore, while endorsing the efforts of the United Nations to bring about a world community favorable to peace, we will work primarily to strengthen the United Nations into a world government of limited powers adequate to prevent a war and *having direct jurisdiction over the individual.*"

The boldness with which liberal Democrats and all "left" organizations discussed their plans for a one-world government alarmed Americans who objected to surrendering their sovereignty and basic right to defend themselves.

Al Snow, Sr.

In 1953, a move was made by the United Nations at the World Federal Government Conference in Copenhagen. They recommended a *revision* of the United Nations Charter to provide for the following:

World citizenship through United Nations Membership with world law applicable to every individual of each member nation.
 1. No right of secession.
 2. That there must be universal membership.
 3. International courts, world legislature, world executive council be established.
 4. That the United Nations be made into a World Federal Government.
 5. Complete and simultaneous disarmament, enforced by United Nations inspection and United Nations police powers.

Later we will look at the United States Department of State Publication 7277 released September 1961 as "Freedom from War," the United States program for general and complete disarmament in a peaceful world and;

Public Law 87-297 87th Congress, H.R. 9118 September 26, 1961 "An Act to Establish a United States Arms Control and Disarmament Agency."

United States Senators ratified the United Nations Charter on July 28, 1945. The vote was 89 YES 2 NO and 5 not voting. Two-thirds of the Senators present concurring therein, the resolution of ratification was agreed to, and the treaty was unconstitutionally ratified.

On the 27th of July 1945, President Truman wrote the Majority Leader, Alben W. Barkley, senior Senator from Kentucky, who had at this time served in the capacity of Majority Leader for a longer period (eight years) of time than anyone else in the history of the Senate. The following is the content of this letter:

The White House
Washington, July 27, 1945

Hon. Alben W. Barkley
The United States Senate,
Washington, D.C.

Dear Alben: Today marks the eighth anniversary of your service as Majority Leader of the Senate. I understand that this is twice as long as any of your predecessors have served. These years have been eventful ones. They have been years of great moment to the United States and to the world.

In all of the recent events which have meant so much in shaping the future of our civilization you have played an important and effective role. Not only have you helped to fulfill the ideals and principles of our party, but you have been willing and anxious to lay aside all semblance of partisanship or desire for party advantage whenever the welfare of our Nation required.

I congratulate you on your past service as Majority Leader, and, also on your 33 years of service in the Congress. The Nation is grateful to you for your patriotic share in the accomplishments of these years, and I know that the years to come will be equally fruitful.

With all best wishes for your continued health and success from your old friend.

Very sincerely yours,
Harry Truman

The Charter of the United Nations was signed on 26 June 1945, in San Francisco, California, at the conclusion of the United Nations Conference on International Organization. It came into force on 24 October 1945.

The Statute of the International Court of Justice is an integral part of the Charter.

Chapter 9
How the U.S. Would Interact with the U.N. "U.N. Participation Act of 1945"

This Act was passed by the Congress December 20, 1945, and amended October 19, 1949. A more correct title would be: "United States Participation in the United Nations Act."

Some constitutional scholars believe this act is Public Law of the United States, and therefore is binding on the Federal Government, as well as the individual States, the same as any other federal law.

> Public Law defines rights and duties with either the operation of government, or the relationships between the government and individuals, associations, and corporations.

To make clear the distinction between "police action," and "war," Congress enacted the United Nations Participation Act of 1945 authorizing the president to negotiate an agreement with the United Nations Security Council, making a limited number of American armed forces, after approval by Congress, available for the United Nations Security Council to use as it sees fit under Article 42 of the Charter of the United Nations.

This was done to make sure that the president did not act unilaterally to place United States armed forces under United Nations command.

It is an enabling act to the United Nations Charter by law, in addition to the treaty-making provision of the Constitution. In the event the question should arise as to whether or not the United Nations Charter is a self-executing treaty, this act settles the question. The United Nations Charter definitely is self-executing because the U.N. Charter needs no court action to make it effective and confer new powers.

> Enabling Act or Statute is the term applied to any act or statute enabling persons or corporations, or agencies to do what before they could not. It is applied to acts or statutes which confer new powers.

> Self Executing Treaty is a treaty which is effective immediately without the need of intervening court action, ancillary legislation, or other type of implementing action.

States Sanctioned and Approved

The question has been raised by some constitutional scholars, when the Federal Government ratified the United Nations Charter –

"Did it include the States with the Federal Government?" The scholars answer is, "YES" under Article 6, Paragraph 2 of the Constitution of the United States, the states were joined with the federal government in the United Nations organization, and their belief is the States are bound by the United Nations Charter.

In addition, by the legislative act of the Congress as above cited, scholars also believe that *state legislatures* automatically sanctioned and approved the United Nations Organization before ratification in 1945.

Therefore, they assert that the United States of America is bound to the United Nations Organization. In addition, they are of the opinion that the United States is bound to all other U.N. treaties and agreements since 1945. Many disagree with this opinion.

Authorizing Executive Orders

Section 5 of the United Nations Participation Act of 1945 is the basic law authorizing the relinquishment of our Sovereignty by U.S. Executive Order No. 10995 through No. 11051, and others. It must be kept in mind that some believe this is not only Public Law of the United States, but it is United Nations Law, as well. Only the Supreme Court of the United States can make that legal determination.

Many are of the opinion that the Executive Orders are without basis of law. When Executive Orders undermine the Constitution, they are null and void, as well as any law that does the same.

Public Law

Some constitutional scholars feel the ratification of the United Nations Charter by the President and Senate, the presumed sanction and approval of the United Nations Organization by the State Legislatures before ratification, and the enactment of the United Nations Participation Act, *made the United Nations Charter Public Law of the Federal Government.*

All other treaties and agreements of the United Nations Organization are Public Law of the Federal Government, and of the States. Read carefully Sections 5 and 6 of the Participation Act.

Remember, this is the question – Is the original treaty with the U.N. constitutional, or not.

Treaty Law

The Supreme Court ruled in Hauenstein v. Lynham (1880) 100 U.S. 483, 25 L. Ed. 628, "It must always be borne in mind that the Constitution, laws, and treaties of the United States are as much a part of the law of *every State* as its own local laws and Constitution. This is a fundamental principle in our system of complex national policy." This decision was made 65 years before the U.N. Organization. However, Treaty Law can be enforced in both Federal and State Courts, *only if they are constitutional*.

The only way to get out from under one-world treaty law and government is to repeal, rescind and revoke the United Nations charter in its entirety.

The mere repeal of the United Nations Participation Act is not sufficient. The basic Treaty must be repealed.

The United Nations Participation Act of 1945, as amended, is published herewith for your information.

UNITED NATIONS PARTICIPATION ACT OF 1945

United Nations Participation Act of 1945, (December 20, 1945)
   As Amended October 19, 1949

AN ACT To provide for the appointment of representatives of the United States in the organs and agencies of the United Nations, and to make other provision with respect to the participation of the United States in such organization.

Be it enacted by the Senate and House of Representatives of the United States of America in Congress assembled, That this Act may be cited as the "United Nations Participation Act of 1945."

Section 2.
(a) The President, by and with the advice and consent of the Senate, shall appoint a representative and a deputy representative of the United States to the United Nations, both of whom shall have the rank and status of envoy extraordinary and ambassador plenipotentiary and shall hold office at the pleasure of the President. Such representative and deputy representative shall represent the United States in the Security Council of the United Nations and may serve ex officio as United States representative on any organ, commission, or other body of the United Nations other than specialized agencies of the United Nations, and shall perform such other functions in connection with the participation of the United States in the United Nations as the President may from time to time direct.

(b) The President, by and with the advice and consent of the Senate, shall appoint an additional deputy representative of the United States to the Security Council who shall hold office at the pleasure of the President. Such deputy representative shall represent the United States in the Security Council of the United Nations in the event of the absence or disability of both the representative and the deputy representative of the United States to the United Nations.

(c) The President, by and with the advice and consent of the Senate, shall designate from time to time to attend a specified session or specified sessions of the General Assembly of the United Nations not to exceed five representatives of the United States and such number of alternates as he may determine consistent with the rules of procedure of the General Assembly. One of the representatives shall be designated as the senior representative.

(d) The President may also appoint from time to time such other persons as he may deem necessary to represent the United States in the organs and agencies of the United Nations, but the representative of the United States in the Economic and Social Council and in the Trusteeship Council of the United Nations shall be appointed only by and with the advice and consent of the Senate, except that the President may, without the advice and consent of the Senate, designate any officer of the United States to act, without additional compensation, as the representative of the United States in either such Council (A) at any specified session thereof where the position is vacant or in the absence or disability of the regular representative, or (B) in connection with a specified matter at any specified session of either such Council in lieu of the regular representative. The President may designate any officer of the Department of State, whose appointment is subject to confirmation by the Senate, to act without additional compensation, for temporary periods as the representative of the United States in the Security Council of the United Nation in the absence or disability of the representative and deputy representative appointed under section 2 (a) or (b) or in lieu of such representatives in connection with a specified subject matter. The advice and consent of the Senate shall be required for the appointed by the President of the representative of the United States in any commission that may be formed by the United Nations with respect to atomic energy or in any other commission of the United Nations to which the United States is entitled to appoint a representative.

(e) Nothing contained in this section shall preclude the President or the Secretary of State, at the direction of the President, from representing the United States at any meeting or session of any organ or agency of the United Nations.

(f) All persons appointed in pursuance of authority contained in this section shall receive compensation at rates determined by the President upon the basis of duties to be performed but not in excess of rates authorized by sections 411 and 412 of the Foreign Service Act of 1946 (Public Law 724, Seventy-ninth Congress) for chiefs of mission and Foreign Service officers occupying positions of equivalent importance, except that no member of the Senate or House of Representatives or officer of the United States who is designated under subsections (c) and (d) of this section as a representative of the United States or as an alternate to attend any specified session or specified sessions of the General Assembly shall be entitled to receive such compensation.

Section 3. The representatives provided for in section 2 hereof, when representing the United States in the respective organs and agencies of the United Nations, shall, at all times, act in accordance with the instructions of the President transmitted by the Secretary of State unless other means of transmission is directed by the President, and such representatives shall, in accordance with such instructions, cast any and all votes under the Charter of the United Nations.

Section 4. The President shall, from time to time as occasion may require, but not less than once each year, make reports to the Congress of the activities of the United Nations and of the participation of the United States therein. He shall make special current reports on decisions of the Security Council to take enforcement measures under the provisions of the Charter of the United Nations, and on the participation therein under his instructions, of the representative of the United States.

Section 5 (a). Notwithstanding the provisions of any other law, whenever the United States is called upon by the Security Council to apply measures which said Council has decided, pursuant to article 41 of said Charter, are to be employed to give effect to its decisions under said Charter, the President may, to the extent necessary to apply such measures, through any agency which he may designate, and under such orders, rules, and regulations as may be prescribed by him, investigate, regulate, or prohibit, in whole or in part, economic relations or rail, sea, postal, telegraphic, radio, and other means of communication between any foreign country or any national thereof or any person therein and the United States or any person subject to the jurisdiction thereof, or involving any property subject to the jurisdiction of the United States.

(b) Any person who willfully violates or evades or attempts to violate or evade an order, rule, or regulation issued by the President pursuant to paragraph (a) of this section shall, upon conviction, be fined not more than $10,000 or, if a natural person, be imprisoned for not more than ten years, or both; and the officer, director, or agent of any corporation, who knowingly participates in such violation or evasion, shall be punished by a like fine, imprisonment, or both, and any property, funds, securities, papers, or other articles or documents, or any vessel, together with her tackle, apparel, furniture and equipment, vehicle or aircraft, concerned in such violation shall be forfeited to the United States.

Section 6. The President is authorized to negotiate a special agreement or agreements with the Security Council which will be subject to the approval of the Congress by appropriate Act or joint resolution, providing for the numbers and types of armed forces, their degree of readiness and general location, and the nature of facilities and assistance, including rights of passage, to be made available to the Security Council on its call for the purpose of maintaining international peace and security in accordance with article 43 of said Charter. The President shall not be deemed to require the authorization of the Congress to make available to the Security Council on its call in order to take action under article 42 of said Charter and pursuant to such special agreement or agreements the armed forces, facilities, or assistance provided for therein Provided, That, except as authorized in section 7 of this Act, nothing herein contained shall be construed as an authorization to the President by the Congress to make available to the Security Council for such purpose armed forces, facilities, or assistance in addition to the forces, facilities, and assistance provided for in such special agreement or agreements.

Section 7 (a). Notwithstanding the provisions of any other law, the President, upon the request by the United Nations for cooperative action, and to the extent that he finds that it is consistent with the national interest to comply with such request, may authorize, in support of such activities of the United Nations as are specifically directed to the peaceful settlement of disputes and not involving the employment of armed forces contemplated by chapter VII of the United Nations Charter –

> (1) the detail to the United Nations, under such terms and conditions as the President shall determine; of personnel of the armed forces of the United States to serve as observers, guards, or in any noncombatant capacity, but in no event shall more than a total of one thousand of such personnel be so detailed at any one time: Provided, That while so detailed, such personnel shall be considered for all purposes as acting in the line of duty, including the receipt of pay and allowances as personnel of the armed forces of the United States, credit for longevity and retirement, and all other perquisites appertaining to such duty: Provided further, That authorization or approval by the President, such personnel may accept directly from the United Nations (a) any or all of the allowances or perquisites to which they are entitled under the first proviso hereof, and (b) extraordinary expenses and perquisites incident to such detail;

(2) the furnishing of facilities, services, or other assistance and the loan of the agreed fair share of the United States of any supplies and equipment to the United Nations by the National Military Establishment, under such terms and conditions as the President shall determine;

(3) the obligation, insofar as necessary to carry out the purposes of clauses (1) and (2) of this subsection, of any funds appropriated to the National Military Establishment or any department therein, the procurement of such personnel, supplies, equipment, facilities, services, or other assistance as may be made available in accordance with the request of the United Nations, and the replacement of such items, when necessary, where they are furnished from stocks.

(b) Whenever personnel or assistance is made available pursuant to the authority contained in subsection (a) (1) and (2) of this section, the President shall require reimbursement from the United Nations for the expense thereby incurred by the United States: Provided, That in exceptional circumstances, or when the President finds it to be in the national interest, he may waive, in whole or in part, the requirement of such reimbursement: Provided further, That when any such reimbursement is made, it shall be credited, at the option of the appropriate department of the National Military Establishment, either to the appropriation, fund, or account utilized in incurring the obligation, or to an appropriate appropriation, fund, or account currently available for the purpose for which expenditures were made.

(c) In addition to the authorization of appropriations to the Department of State contained in section 8 of this Act, there is hereby authorized to be appropriated to the National Military Establishment, or any department therein, such sums as may be necessary to reimburse such Establishment or department in the event that reimbursement from the United Nations is waived in whole or in part pursuant to authority contained in subsection (b) of this section.

(d) Nothing in this Act shall authorize the disclosure of any information or knowledge in any case in which such disclosure is prohibited by any other law of the United States.

Section 8. There is hereby authorized to be appropriated annually to the Department of State, out of any money in the Treasury not otherwise appropriated, such sums as may be necessary for the payment by the United States of its share of the expenses of the United Nations as apportioned by the General Assembly in accordance with article 17 of the Charter, and for all necessary salaries and expenses of the representatives provided in section 2 hereof, and of their appropriate staffs, including personal services in the District of Columbia and elsewhere, without regard to the civil-service laws and the Classification Act of 1923, as amended; travel expenses without regard to the Standardized Government Travel Regulations, as amended, the Travel Expense Act of 1949, and section 10 of the Act of March 3, 1933, as amended, and, under such rules and regulations as the Secretary of State may prescribe, travel expenses of families and transportation of effects of United States representatives and other personnel in going to and returning from their post of duty; allowances for living quarters, including heat, fuel, and light, as authorized by the Act approved June 26, 1930 (5 U.S. C. 118a); cost-of-living allowances for personnel stationed abroad under such rules and regulations as the Secretary of State may prescribe; communications services; stenographic reporting, translating, and other services by contract; hire of passenger motor vehicles and other local transportation; rent of offices; printing and binding without regard to section 11 of the Act of March 1, 1919 (44 U.S. C. 111); allowances and expenses as provided in section 6 of the Act of July 30, 1946 (Public Law 565, Seventy-ninth Congress), and allowances and expenses equivalent to those provided in section 901 (3) of the Foreign Service Act of 1946 (Public Law 724, Seventy-ninth Congress); the lease and rental (for periods not exceeding ten years) of living quarters for the use of the representative of the United States to the United Nations referred to in paragraph (a) of section 2 hereof, the cost of installation and use of telephones in the same manner as telephone service is provided for use of the Foreign Service pursuant to the Act of August 23, 1912, as amended (31 U.S. C. 679), and the allotment of funds, similar to the allotment authorized by section 902 of the Foreign Service Act of 1946, for unusual expenses incident to the operation and maintenance of such living quarters, to be accounted for in accordance with section 903 of said Act; and such other expenses as may be authorized by the Secretary of State; all without regard to section 3709 of the Revised Statutes, as amended (41 U.S. C. 5).

Reid v. Covert, 354 U.S. 1 (1957)

This case stated: "It would be manifestly contrary to the objectives of those who created the Constitution ... let alone alien to our entire Constitution history and tradition to construe article VI (The Supremacy Clause) as permitting the United States to exercise power under an international agreement without observing Constitutional prohibitions. In effect, such construction would permit amendment of that document in a manner not sanctioned by article V."

Remembering George Washington's warnings, "One method of assault may be to effect, in the forms of the Constitution, alterations which will impair the energy of the system, and thus to undermine what cannot be directly overthrown..."

This is exactly what the U.N. Charter does. It makes alterations to the U.S. Constitution and thus it undermines the Constitution, a document which cannot be *directly* overthrown.

Chapter 10
Proposals for New Disarmament Program Speech by John F. Kennedy to U.N., 1961

FUTURE OF THE UNITED NATIONS ORGANIZATION
Proposals for New Disarmament Program
By: John F. Kennedy, President of the United States
Delivered to the United Nations General Assembly, United Nations, New York
September 25, 1961

I. We meet in an hour of grief and challenge. Dag Hammarskjold (Sec-General of U.N.) is dead. But the United Nations lives. His tragedy is deep in our hearts, but the task for which he died is at the top of our agenda. A noble servant of peace is gone. But the quest for peace lies before us.

The problem is not the death of one man – the problem is the life of this organization. It will either grow to meet the challenges of our age, or it will be gone with the wind, without influence, without force, without respect. Were we to let it die, to enfeeble its vigor, to cripple its powers, we would condemn our future.

For in the development of this organization rests the only true alternative to war – and war appeals no longer as a rational alternative. Unconditional war can no longer lead to unconditional victory. It can no longer serve to settle disputes. It can no longer concern the great powers alone. For a nuclear disaster, spread by wind and water and fear, could well engulf the great and the small, the rich and the poor, the committed and the uncommitted alike. Mankind must put an end to war – or war will put an end to mankind.

So let us here resolve that Dag Hammarskjold did not live, or die, in vain. Let us call a truce to terror. Let us invoke the blessings of peace. And as we build an international capacity to keep peace, let us join in dismantling the national capacity to wage war.

II. This will require new strength and new roles for the United Nations. For disarmament without checks is but a shadow – and a community without law is but a shell. Already the United Nations has become both the measure and the vehicle of man's most generous impulses. Already it has provided – in the Middle East, in Asia, in Africa this year in the Congo – a means of holding man's violence within bounds.

But the great question which confronted this body in 1945 is still before us: whether man's cherished hopes for progress and peace are to be destroyed by terror and disruption, whether the "foul winds of war" can be tamed in time to free the cooling winds of reason, and whether the pledges of our Charter are to be fulfilled or defied – pledges to secure peace, progress, human rights and world law.

In this Hall, there are not three forces, but two. One is composed of those who are trying to build the kind of world described in Articles I and II of the Charter. The other, seeking a far different world, would undermine this organization in the process.

Today, of all days our dedication to the Charter must be maintained. It must be strengthened first of all by the election of an outstanding civil servant to carry forward the responsibilities of the Secretary General – a man endowed with both the wisdom and the power to make meaningful the moral force of the world community. The late Secretary General nurtured and sharpened the United Nations' obligation to act. But he did not invent it. It was there in the Charter. It is still there in the Charter.

However difficult it may be to fill Mr. Hammarskjold's place, it can better be filled by one man rather than three. Even the three horses of the Troika did not have three drivers, all going in different directions. They had only one – and so must the United Nations executive. To install a triumvirate, or any panel, or any rotating authority, in the United Nations administrative offices would replace order with anarchy, action with paralysis, confidence with confusion.

The Secretary General, in a very real sense, is the servant of the General Assembly. Diminish his authority and you diminish the authority of the only body where all nations, regardless of power, are equal and sovereign. Until all the powerful are just, the weak will be secure only in the strength of this Assembly.

Effective and independent executive action is not the same question as balanced representation. In view of the enormous change in membership in this body since its founding, the United States delegation will join in any effort for the prompt review and revision of the composition of United Nations bodies.

But to give this organization three drivers – to permit each great power to decide its own case, would entrench the Cold War in the headquarters of peace. Whatever advantages such a plan may hold out to my own country, as one of the great powers, we reject it. For we far prefer world law, in the age of self-determination, to world war, in the age of mass extermination.

III. Today, every inhabitant of this planet must contemplate the day when this planet may no longer be habitable. Every man, woman and child lives under a nuclear sword of Damocles, hanging by the slenderest of threads, capable of being cut at any moment by accident or miscalculation or by madness. The weapons of war must be abolished before they abolish us.

Men no longer debate whether armaments are a symptom or a cause of tension. The mere existence of modern weapons – ten million times more powerful than any that the world has ever seen, and only minutes away from any target on earth – is a source of horror, and discord and distrust. Men no longer maintain that disarmament must await the settlement of all disputes – for disarmament must be a part of any permanent settlement. And men may no longer pretend that the quest for disarmament is a sign of weakness – for in a spiraling arms race, a nation's security may well be shrinking even as its arms increase.

For fifteen years this organization has sought the reduction and destruction of arms. Now that goal is no longer a dream – it is a practical matter of life or death. The risks inherent in disarmament pale in comparison to the risks inherent in an unlimited arms race.

It is in this spirit that the recent Belgrade Conference – recognizing that this is no longer a Soviet problem or an American problem, but a human problem – endorsed a program of "general, complete and strictly an internationally controlled disarmament." It is in this same spirit that we in the United States have labored this year, with a new urgency, and with a new, now statutory agency fully endorsed by the Congress, to find an approach to disarmament which would be so far-reaching, yet realistic, so mutually balanced and beneficial, that it could be accepted by every nation. And it is in this spirit that we have presented with the agreement of the Soviet Union – under the label both nations now accept of "general and complete disarmament" – a new statement of newly-agreed principles for negotiation.

But we are well aware that all issues of principle are not settled, and that principles alone are not enough. It is therefore our intention to challenge the Soviet Union, not to an arms race, but to a peace race – to advance together step by step, stage by stage, until general and complete disarmament has been achieved. We invite them now to go beyond agreement in principle to reach agreement on actual plans.

The program to be presented to this assembly – for general and complete disarmament under effective international control – moves to bridge the gap between those who insist on a gradual approach and those who talk only of the final and total achievement. It would create machinery to keep the peace as it destroys the machinery of war. It would proceed through balanced and safeguarded stages designed to give no state a military advantage over another. It would place the final responsibility for verification and control where it belongs, not with the big powers alone, not with one's adversary or one's self, but in an international organization within the framework of the United Nations. It would assure that indispensable condition of disarmament – true inspection – and apply it in stages proportionate to the stage of disarmament. It would cover delivery systems as well as weapons. It would ultimately halt their production as well as their testing, their transfer as well as their possession. It would achieve under the eyes of an international disarmament organization, a steady reduction in force, both nuclear and conventional, until it has abolished all armies and all weapons except those needed for internal order and a new United Nations Peace Force. And it starts that process now, today, even as the talk begin.

In short, general and complete disarmament must no longer be a slogan, used to resist the first steps. It is no longer to be a goal without means of achieving it, without means of verifying its progress, without means of keeping the peace. It is now a realistic plan, and a test – a test of those only willing to talk and a test of those willing to act.

Such a plan would not bring a world free from conflict and greed – but it would bring a world free from the terrors of mass destruction. It would not usher in the era of the super state – but it would usher in an era in which no state could annihilate or be annihilated by another.

In 1946, this Nation proposed the Baruch Plan to internationalize the atom before other nations even possessed the bomb or demilitarized their troops. We proposed with our allies the Disarmament plan of 1951 while still at war in Korea. And we make our proposals today, while building up our defenses over Berlin, not because we are inconsistent or insincere or intimidated, but because we know the rights of free men will prevail – because while we are compelled against our will to rearm, we look confidently beyond Berlin to the kind of disarmed world we all prefer.

I therefore propose on the basis of this Plan, that disarmament negotiations resume promptly, and continue without interruption until an entire program for general and complete disarmament has not only been agreed upon but has actually been achieved.

IV. The logical place to begin is a treaty assuring the end of nuclear tests of all kinds, in every environment, under workable controls. The United States and the United Kingdom have proposed such a treaty that is both reasonable, effective and ready for signature. We are still prepared to sign that treaty today.

We also proposed a mutual ban on atmospheric testing, without inspection or control, in order to save the human race from the poison of radioactive fallout. We regret that the offer has not been accepted.

For 15 years we have sought to make the atom an instrument of peaceful growth rather than of war. But the 15 years our concessions have been matched by obstruction, our patience by intransigence. And the pleas of mankind for peace have met with disregard.

Finally, as the explosions of others beclouded the skies, my country was left with no alternative but to act in its own interests and in the interests of the free world's security. We cannot endanger that security by refraining from testing while others improve their arsenal. Nor can we endanger it by another long, uninspected ban on testing. For three years, we accepted those risks in our open society while seeking agreement on inspection. But this year, while we were negotiating in good faith in Geneva, others were secretly preparing new experiments in destruction.

Our tests are not polluting the atmosphere. Our deterrent weapons are guarded against accidental explosion or use. Our doctors and scientists stand ready to help any nation measure and meet the hazards to health which inevitably result from the tests in the atmosphere.

But to halt the spread of these terrible weapons, to halt the contamination of the air, to halt the spiraling nuclear arms race, we remain ready to seek new avenues of agreement, our new Disarmament Program thus includes the following proposals:

—First, signing the test-ban treaty by all nations. This can be done now. Test ban negotiations need not and should not await general disarmament.

—Second, stopping the production of fissionable materials for use in weapons, and preventing their transfer to any nation now lacking in nuclear weapons.

—Third, prohibiting the transfer of control over nuclear weapons to states that do not own them.

—Fourth, keeping nuclear weapons from seeding new battlegrounds in outer space.

Exceptional Profile of Courage

—Fifth, gradually destroying existing nuclear weapons and converting their materials to peaceful uses; and

—Finally, halting the unlimited testing and production of strategic nuclear delivery vehicles, and gradually destroying them as well.

V. To destroy arms, however, is not enough. We must create even as we destroy – creating worldwide law and law enforcement as we outlaw worldwide war and weapons. In the world we seek, the United Nations Emergency Forces which have been hastily assembled, uncertainly supplied, and inadequately financed, will never be enough.

Therefore, the United States recommends that all member nations earmark special peace-keeping units in their armed forces – to be on call to the United Nations, to be specially trained and quickly available, and with advanced provision for financial and logistic support.

In addition, the American delegation will suggest a series of steps to improve the United Nations' machinery for the peaceful settlement of disputes – for on-the-spot fact-finding, mediation and adjudication – for extending the rule of international law. For peace is not solely a matter of military or technical problems – it is primarily a problem of politics and people. And unless man can match his strides in weapons and technology with equal strides in social and political development, our great strength, like that of the dinosaur, will become incapable of proper control – and, like the dinosaur, will vanish from the earth.

VI. As we extend the rule of law on earth, so must we also extend it to man's new domain – outer space.

All of us salute the brave cosmonauts of the Soviet Union. The new horizons of outer space must not be riven by the old bitter concepts of imperialism and sovereign claims. The cold reaches of the universe must not become the new arena of an even colder war.

To this end, we shall urge proposals extending the United Nations Charter to the limits of man's exploration in the universe, reserving outer space for peaceful use, prohibiting weapons of mass destruction in space or on celestial bodies, and opening the mysteries and benefits of space to every nation. We shall propose further cooperative efforts between all the nations in weather prediction and eventually in weather control. We shall propose, finally, a global system of communications satellites linking the whole world in telegraph and telephone and radio and television. The day need not be far away when such a system will televise the proceedings of this body to every corner of the world for the benefit of peace.

VII. But the mysteries of outer space must not divert our eyes or our energies from the harsh realities that face our fellow men. Political sovereignty is but a mockery without the means of meeting poverty, illiteracy, and disease. Self-determination is but a slogan if the future holds no hope.

That is why my nation, which has freely shared its capital and its technology to help others help themselves, now proposes officially designating this decade of the 1960s as the United Nations Decade of Development. Under the framework of that Resolution, the United Nations' existing efforts in promoting economic growth can be expanded and coordinated. Regional surveys and training institutes can now pool the talents of many. New research, technical assistance and pilot projects can unlock the wealth of less developed lands and untapped waters. And development can become a cooperative and not a competitive enterprise – to enable all nations, however diverse in their systems and beliefs, to become in fact as well as in law both free and equal nations.

VIII. My country favors world of free and equal states. We agree with those who say that colonialism is a key issue in this Assembly. But let the full facts of that issue be discussed in full.

On the one hand is the fact that, since the close of World War II, a worldwide declaration of independence has transformed nearly 1 billion people and 9 million square miles into 42 free and independent states. Less than 2 percent of the world's population now lives in "dependent" territories.

I do not ignore the remaining problems of traditional colonialism, which still confront this body. Those problems will be solved, with patience, good will, and determination. Within the limits of our responsibility in such matters, my country intends to be a participant and not merely an observer, in the peaceful, expeditious movement of nations from the status of colonies to the partnership of equals. That continuing tide of self-determination, which runs so strong, has our sympathy and our support.

But colonialism in its harshest forms is not only the exploitation of new nations by old, of dark skins by light, or the subjugation of the poor by the rich. My Nation was once a colony, and we know what colonialism means; the exploitation and subjugation of the weak by the powerful, of the many by the few, of the governed who have given no consent to be governed, whatever their continent, their class, or their color.

And that is why there is no ignoring the fact that the tide of self-determination has not yet reached the Communist empire where a population far larger than that officially termed "dependent" lives under governments installed by foreign troops instead of free institutions – under a system which knows only one party and one belief – which suppresses free debate, and free elections, and free newspapers, and free books, and free trade unions – and which builds a wall to keep truth a stranger and its own citizens prisoners. Let us debate colonialism in full – and apply the principle of free choice and the practice of free plebiscites in every corner of the globe.

IX. Finally, as President of the United States, I consider it my duty to report to this Assembly on two threats to the peace which are not on your crowded agenda, but which cause us and most of you, the deepest concern.

The first threat on which I wish to report is widely misunderstood: the smoldering coals of war in Southeast Asia. South Vietnam is already under attack – sometimes by a single assassin, sometimes by a band of guerrillas, recently by full battalions. The peaceful borders of Burma, Cambodia, and India have been repeatedly violated. And the peaceful people of Laos are in danger of losing the independence they gained not so long ago.

No one can call these "wars of liberation." For these are free countries living under their own governments. Nor are these aggressions any less real because men are knifed in their homes and not shot in the fields of battle.

The very simple question confronting the world community is whether measures can be devised to protect the small and the weak from such tactics. For if they are successful in Laos and South Vietnam, the gates will be opened wide.

The United States seeks for itself, no base, no territory, no special position in this area of any kind. We support a truly neutral and independent Laos, its people free from outside interference, living at peace with themselves and with their neighbors, assured that their territory will not be used for attacks on others, and under a government comparable (as Mr. Khrushchev and I agreed at Vienna) to Cambodia and Burma.

But now the negotiations over Laos are reaching a crucial stage. The cease-fire is at best precarious. The rainy season is coming to an end. Laotian territory is being used to infiltrate South Vietnam. The world community must recognize – and all those who are involved – that this potent threat to Laotian peace and freedom is indivisible from all other threats to their own.

Secondly, I wish to report to you on the crisis over Germany and Berlin. This is not the time or the place for immoderate tones, but the world community is entitled to know the very simple issues as we see them. If there is a crisis it is because an existing peace in that area is under threat, because an existing island of free people is under pressure, because solemn agreements are being treated with indifference. Established international rights are being threatened with unilateral usurpation. Peaceful circulation has been interrupted by barbed wire and concrete blocks.

One recalls the order of the Czar in Pushkin's [1825 play] "Boris Godunov:"

"Take steps at this very hour that our frontiers be fenced by barriers….That not a single soul pass o'er the border, that not a hare be able to run or a crow fly."

It is absurd to allege that we are threatening a war merely to prevent the Soviet Union and East Germany from signing a so-called "treaty" of peace. The Western Allies are not concerned with any paper arrangement the Soviets may wish to make with a regime of their own creation, on territory occupied by their own troops and governed by their own agents. No such action can, however, affect either our rights or our responsibilities.

If there is a dangerous crisis in Berlin – and there is – it is because of threats against the vital interests and the deep commitments of the Western Powers, and the freedom of West Berlin. We cannot yield these interests. We cannot fail these commitments. We cannot surrender the freedom of these people for whom we are responsible. A "peace-treaty" which carried with it the provisions which destroy the peace would be a fraud.. A "free city" which was not genuinely free would suffocate freedom and would be an infamy.

For a city or a people to be truly free they must have the secure right, without economic, political or police pressure, to make their own choice and to live their own lives. And as I have said before, if anyone doubts the extent to which our presence is desired by the people of West Berlin, we are ready to have that question submitted to a free vote in all Berlin and, if possible, among all the German people.

The elementary fact about this crisis is that it is unnecessary. The elementary tools for a peaceful settlement are to be found in the Charter. Under its law, agreements are to be kept, unless changed by all those who made them. Established rights are to be respected. The political disposition of peoples should rest upon their own wishes, freely expressed in plebiscites or free elections. If there are legal problems, they can be solved by legal means. If there is a threat of force, it must be rejected. If there is a desire for change, it must be a subject for negotiation, and if there is negotiation, it must be rooted in mutual respect and concern for the rights of others.

The Western Powers have calmly resolved to defend, by whatever means are forced upon them, their obligations and their access to the free citizens of West Berlin and the self-determination of those citizens. This generation learned from bitter experience that either brandishing or yielding to threats can only lead to war. But firmness and reason can lead to the kind of peaceful solution in which my country profoundly believes.

We are committed to no rigid formula. We see no perfect solution. We recognize that troops and tanks can, for a time, keep a nation divided against its will, however, unwise that policy may seem to us. But we believe a peaceful agreement is possible which protects the freedom of West Berlin and allied presence and access, while recognizing the historic and legitimate interests of others in insuring European security.

The possibilities of negotiation are now being explored; it is too early to report what the prospects may be. For our part, we would be glad to report at the appropriate time that a solution has been found. For there is no need for a crisis over Berlin, threatening the peace-and if those who created this crisis desire peace, there will be peace and freedom in Berlin.

X. The events and decisions of the next ten months may well decide the fate of man for the next ten thousand years. There will be no avoiding these events. There will be no appeal from these decisions. And we in this hall shall be remembered either as part of the generation that turned this planet into a flaming funeral pyre or the generation that met its vow "to save succeeding generations from the scourge of war."

In the endeavor to meet that vow, I pledge you every effort that this Nation possesses. I pledge you that we shall neither commit nor provoke aggression, that we shall neither flee nor invoke the threat of force, that we shall never negotiate out of fear, and we shall never fear to negotiate.

Terror is not a new weapon. Throughout history it has been used by those who could not prevail, either by persuasion or by example. But inevitably they fail, either because men are not afraid to die for a life worth living, or because the terrorists themselves came to realize that free men cannot be frightened by threats, and that aggression would meet its own response. And it is in the light of that history that every nation today should know, be it friend or foe, that the United States has both the will and the weapons to join free men in standing up to their responsibilities.

But I come here today to look across this world of threats to a world at peace. In that search we cannot expect any final triumph – for new problems will always arise. We cannot expect

Exceptional Profile of Courage

that all nations will adopt like systems – for conformity is the jailer of freedom, and the enemy of growth. Nor can we expect to reach our goal by contrivance, by fiat or even by the wishes of all.

But however close we sometimes seem to that dark and final abyss, let no man of peace and freedom despair. For he does not stand alone. If we all can persevere, if we can in every land and office look beyond our own shores and ambitions, then surely the age will dawn in which the strong are just and the weak secure and the peace preserved.

Ladies and gentlemen of this Assembly, the decision is ours. Never have the nations of the world had so much to lose, or so much to gain. Together we shall save our planet, or together we shall perish in its flames. Save it we can – and save it we must – and then shall we earn the eternal thanks of mankind and, as peacemakers, the eternal blessing of God. (End of speech)

2001 Update. President Dwight Eisenhower signed the "Open Skies" treaty which allows foreign military aircraft to fly over the United States.

President Ronald Reagan signed the "Intermediate Nuclear Force Treaty" with Boris Yeltsin which allows the Russians to monitor the destruction of U.S.-owned weapons on American soil.

Every president since Franklin Delano Roosevelt has participated in the disarmament program.

Those very proposals for new disarmament are in violation with the United States Constitution and the Bill of Rights Second Amendment. No president has the constitutional power to disarm the United States government and/or the United States citizens. The president took an oath to uphold and protect the U.S. Constitution.

Chapter 11
"Freedom from War–the United States Program for General and Complete Disarmament in a Peaceful World."
U. S. Department of State Publication 7277

During John Kennedy's address to the United Nations General Assembly on September 25, 1961, he presented the policy book – Publication 7277 "Freedom from War–the United States Program for General and Complete Disarmament in a Peaceful World." This is what it says.

INTRODUCTION

The revolutionary development of modern weapons within a world divided by serious ideological differences has produced a crisis in human history. In order to overcome the danger of nuclear war now confronting mankind, the United States has introduced at the Sixteenth General Assembly of the United Nations a Program for General and Complete Disarmament in a Peaceful World.

This new program provides for the progressive reduction of the war-making capabilities of nations and the simultaneous strengthening of international institutions to settle disputes and maintain the peace. It sets forth a series of comprehensive measures which can and should be taken in order to bring about a world in which there will be freedom from war and security for all states. It is based on three principles deemed essential to the achievement of practical progress in the disarmament field:

FIRST, THERE MUST BE IMMEDIATE DISARMAMENT ACTION

A strenuous and uninterrupted effort must be made toward the goal of general and complete disarmament; at the same time, it is important that specific measures be put into effect as soon as possible.

SECOND, ALL DISARMAMENT OBLIGATIONS MUST BE SUBJECT TO EFFECTIVE INTERNATIONAL CONTROLS

The control organization must have the manpower, facilities, and effectiveness to assure that limitations or reductions take place as agreed. It must also be able to certify to all states that retained forces and armaments do not exceed those permitted at any stage of the disarmament process.

THIRD, ADEQUATE PEACE-KEEPING MACHINERY MUST BE ESTABLISHED

There is an inseparable relationship between the scaling down of national armaments on the one hand and the building up of international peace-keeping machinery and institutions on the other. Nations are unlikely to shed their means of self-protection in the absence of alternative ways to safeguard their legitimate interests. This can only be achieved through the progressive strengthening of international institutions under the United Nations and by creating a United Nations Peace Force to enforce the peace as the disarmament process proceeds.

FREEDOM FROM WAR

The United States Program for General and Complete Disarmament in a Peaceful World

SUMMARY

Disarmament Goal and Objectives

The over-all goal of the United States is a free, secure, and peaceful world of independent states adhering to common standards of justice and international conduct and subjecting the use of force to the rule of law; a world which has achieved general and complete disarmament under effective international control;

and a world in which adjustment to change takes place in accordance with the principles of the United Nations.

In order to make possible the achievement of that goal, the program sets forth the following specific objectives toward which nations should direct their efforts:

> The disbanding of all national armed forces and the prohibition of their reestablishment in any form whatsoever other than those required to preserve internal order and for contributions to a United Nations Peace Force;
>
> The elimination from national arsenals of all armaments, including all weapons of mass destruction and the means for their delivery, other than those required for a United Nations Peace Force and for maintaining internal order;
>
> The institution of effective means for the enforcement of international agreements, for the settlement of disputes, and for the maintenance of peace in accordance with the principles of the United Nations;
>
> The establishment and effective operation of an International Disarmament Organization within the framework of the United Nations to insure compliance at all times with all disarmament obligations.

TASK OF NEGOTIATING STATES

The negotiating states are called upon to develop the program into a detailed plan for general and complete disarmament and to continue their efforts without interruption until the whole program has been achieved. To this end, they are to seek the widest possible area of agreement at the earliest possible date. At the same time, and without prejudice to progress on the disarmament program, they are to seek agreement on those immediate measures that would contribute to the common security of nations and that could facilitate and form part of the total program.

GOVERNING PRINCIPLES

The program sets forth a series of general principles to guide the negotiating states in their work. These make clear that:

- As states relinquish their arms, the United Nations must be progressively strengthened in order to improve its capacity to assure international security and the peaceful settlement of disputes;
- Disarmament must proceed as rapidly as possible, until it is completed, in stages containing balanced, phased, and safeguarded measures;
- Each measure and stage should be carried out in an agreed period of time, with transition from one stage to the next to take place as soon as all measures in the preceding stage have been carried out and verified and as soon as necessary arrangements for verification of the next stage have been made;
- Inspection and verification must establish both that nations carry out scheduled limitations or reductions and that they do not retain armed forces and armaments in excess of those permitted at any stage of the disarmament process; and
- Disarmament must take place in a manner that will not affect adversely the security of any state.

DISARMAMENT STAGES

The program provides for progressive disarmament steps to take place in three stages and for the simultaneous strengthening of international institutions.

FIRST STAGE

The first stage contains measures which would significantly reduce the capabilities of nations to wage aggressive war. Implementation of this stage would mean that:

The nuclear threat would be reduced

- All states would have adhered to a treaty effectively prohibiting the testing of nuclear weapons.

- The production of fissionable materials for use in weapons would be stopped and quantities of such materials from past production would be converted to non-weapons uses.
- States owning nuclear weapons would not relinquish control of such weapons to any nation not owning them and would not transmit to any such nation information or material necessary for their manufacture.
- States not owning nuclear weapons would not manufacture them or attempt to obtain control of such weapons belonging to other states.
- A Commission of Experts would be established to report on the feasibility and means for the verified reduction and eventual elimination of nuclear weapons stockpiles.

Strategic delivery vehicles would be reduced

Strategic nuclear weapons delivery vehicles of specified categories and weapons designed to counter such vehicles would be reduced to agreed levels by equitable and balanced steps; their production would be discontinued or limited; their testing would be limited or halted.

Arms and armed forces would be reduced

The armed forces of the United States and the Soviet Union would be limited to 2.1 million men each (with appropriate levels not exceeding that amount for other militarily significant states); levels of armaments would be correspondingly reduced and their production would be limited.

An Experts Commission would be established to examine and report on the feasibility and means of accomplishing verifiable reduction and eventual elimination of all chemical, biological and radiological weapons.

Peaceful use of outer space would be promoted

The placing in orbit or stationing in outer space of weapons capable of producing mass destruction would be prohibited.

States would give advance notification of space vehicle and missile launchings.

U.N. peace-keeping powers would be strengthened

Measures would be taken to develop and strengthen United Nations arrangements for arbitration, for the development of international law, and for the establishment in Stage II of a permanent U.N. Peace Force.

An International Disarmament Organization would be established for effective verification of the disarmament program

Its functions would be expanded progressively as disarmament proceeds.

It would certify to all states that agreed reductions have taken place and that retained forces and armaments do not exceed permitted levels.

It would determine the transition from one stage to the next.

States would be committed to other measures to reduce international tension and to protect against the chance of war by accident, miscalculation, or surprise attack

States would be committed to refrain from the threat or use of any type of armed force contrary to the principles of the U.N. Charter and to refrain from indirect aggression and subversion against any country.

An U.N. peace observation group would be available to investigate any situation which might constitute a threat to or breach of the peace.

States would be committed to give advance notice of major military movements which might cause alarm; observation posts would be established to report on concentrations and movements of military forces.

SECOND STAGE

The second stage contains a series of measures which would bring within sight a world in which there would be freedom from war. Implementation of all measures in the second stage would mean:
- Further substantial reductions in the armed forces, arma-

ments, and military establishments of states, including strategic nuclear weapons delivery vehicles and countering weapons;
- Further development of methods for the peaceful settlement of disputes under the United Nations;
- Establishment of a permanent international peace force within the United Nations;
- Depending on the findings of an Experts Commission, a halt in the production of chemical, bacteriological, and radiological weapons and a reduction of existing stocks or their conversion to peaceful uses;
- On the basis of the findings of an Experts Commission, a reduction of stocks of nuclear weapons;
- The dismantling or the conversion to peaceful uses of certain military bases and facilities wherever located; and
- The strengthening and enlargement of the International Disarmament Organization to enable it to verify the steps taken in Stage II and to determine the transition to Stage III.

THIRD STAGE

During the third stage of the program, the states of the world, building on the experience and confidence gained in successfully implementing the measures of the first two stages, would take final steps toward the goal of a world in which:

> States would retain only those forces, non-nuclear armaments, and establishments required for the purpose of maintaining internal order; they would also support and provide agreed manpower for a U.N. Peace Force.

> The U.N. Peace Force, equipped with agreed types and quantities of armaments, would be fully functioning.

> The manufacture of armaments would be prohibited except for those of agreed types and quantities to be used by the U.N. Peace Force and those required to maintain internal order. All other armaments would be destroyed or converted to peaceful purposes.

The peace-keeping capabilities of the United Nations would be sufficiently strong and the obligations of all states under such arrangements sufficiently far-reaching as to assure peace and the just settlement of differences in a disarmed world.

Appendix

DECLARATION ON DISARMAMENT
The United States Program for General and Complete Disarmament in a Peaceful World

The Nations of the world,
Conscious of the crisis in human history produced by the revolutionary development of modern weapons within world divided by serious ideological differences;
Determined to save present and succeeding generations from the scourge of war and the dangers and burdens of the arms race and to create conditions in which all peoples can strive freely and peacefully to fulfill their basic aspirations;
Declare their goal to be: A free, secure, and peaceful world of independent states adhering to common standards of justice and international conduct and subjecting the use of force to the rule of law; a world where adjustment to change takes place in accordance with the principles of the United Nations; a world where there shall be a permanent state of general and complete disarmament under effective international control and where the resources of nations shall be devoted to man's material, cultural, and spiritual advance;
Set forth as the objectives of program of general and complete disarmament in a peaceful world:

(a) The disbanding of all national armed forces and the prohibition of their reestablishment in any form whatsoever other than those required to preserve internal order and for contributions to a United Nations Peace Force;

(b) The elimination from national arsenals of all armaments, including all weapons of mass destruction and the means for

111

their delivery, other than those required for a United Nations Peace Force and for maintaining internal order;

(c) The establishment and effective operation of an International Disarmament Organization within the framework of the United Nations to ensure compliance at all times with all disarmament obligations;

(d) The institution of effective means for the enforcement of international agreements, for the settlement of disputes, and for the maintenance of peace in accordance with the principles of the United Nations.

Call on the negotiating states

(a) To develop the outline program set forth below into an agreed plan for general and complete disarmament and to continue their efforts without interruption until the whole program has been achieved;

(b) To this end to seek to attain the widest possible area of agreement at the earliest possible date;

(c) Also to seek – without prejudice to progress on the disarmament program – agreement on those immediate measures that would contribute to the common security of nations and that could facilitate and form a part of that program.

Affirm that disarmament negotiations should be guided by the following principles

(a) Disarmament shall take place as rapidly as possible until it is completed in stages containing balanced, phased and safeguarded measures, with each measure and stage to be carried out in an agreed period of time.

(b) Compliance with all disarmament obligations shall be effectively verified from their entry into force. Verification arrangements shall be instituted progressively and in such a manner as to verify not only that agreed limitations or reductions take place but also that retained armed forces and armaments do not exceed agreed levels at any stage.

(c) Disarmament shall take place in a manner that will not affect adversely the security of any state, whether or not a party to an international agreement or treaty.

(d) As states relinquish their arms, the United Nations shall be progressively strengthened in order to improve its capacity to assure international security and the peaceful settlement of differences as well as to facilitate the development of international cooperation in common tasks for the benefit of mankind.

(e) Transition from one stage of disarmament to the next shall take place as soon as all the measures in the preceding stage have been carried out and effective verification is continuing and as soon as the arrangements that have been agreed to be necessary for the next stage have been instituted.

Agree upon the following outline program for achieving general and complete disarmament:

STAGE I
A. To Establish an International Disarmament Organization:

(a) An International Disarmament Organization (IDO) shall be established within the framework of the United Nations upon entry into force of the agreement. Its functions shall be expanded progressively as required for the effective verification of the disarmament program.

(b) The IDO shall have: (1) a General Conference of all the parties; (2) a Commission consisting of representatives of all the major powers as permanent members and certain other states on a rotating basis; and (3) an Administrator who will administer the Organization subject to the direction of the Commission and who will have the authority, staff, and finances adequate to assure effective impartial implementation of the functions of the Organization.

(c) The IDO shall: (1) ensure compliance with the obligations undertaken by verifying the execution of measures agreed upon; (2) assist the states in developing the details of agreed further verification and disarmament measures; (3)

provide for the establishment of such bodies as may be necessary for working out the details of further measures provided for in the program and for such other expert study groups as may be required to give continuous study to the problems of disarmament; (4) receive reports on the progress of disarmament and verification arrangements and determine the transition from one stage to the next.

B. To Reduce Armed Forces and Armaments

(a) Force levels shall be limited to 2.1 million each for the U. S. and U.S.S.R. and to appropriate levels not exceeding 2.1 million each for all other militarily significant states. Reductions to the agreed levels will proceed by equitable, proportionate, and verified steps.

(b) Levels of armaments of prescribed types shall be reduced by equitable and balanced steps. The reductions shall be accomplished by transfers of armaments to depots supervised by the IDO. When, at specified periods during the Stage I reduction process, the states party to the agreement have agreed that the armaments and armed forces are at prescribed levels the armaments in depots shall be destroyed or converted to peaceful uses.

(c) The production of agreed types of armaments shall be limited.

(d) A Chemical, Biological, Radiological (CBR) Experts Commission shall be established within the IDO for the purpose of examining and reporting on the feasibility and means for accomplishing the verifiable reduction and eventual elimination of CBR weapons stockpiles and the halting of their production.

C. To Contain and Reduce the Nuclear Threat

(a) States that have not acceded to a treaty effectively prohibiting the testing of nuclear weapons shall do so.

(b) The production of fissionable materials for use in weapons shall be stopped.

(c) Upon the cessation of production of fissionable materials for use in weapons, agreed initial quantities of fissionable materials from past production shall be transferred to non-weapons purposes.

(d) Any fissionable materials transferred between countries for peaceful uses of nuclear energy shall be subject to appropriate safeguards to be developed in agreement with the IAEA.

(e) States owning nuclear weapons shall not relinquish control of such weapons to any nation not owning them and shall not transmit to any such nation information or material necessary for their manufacture. States not owning nuclear weapons shall not manufacture such weapons, attempt to obtain control of such weapons belonging to other states, or seek or receive information or materials necessary for their manufacture.

(f) A Nuclear Experts Commission consisting of representatives of the nuclear states shall be established within the IDO for the purpose of examining and reporting on the feasibility and means for accomplishing the verified reduction and eventual elimination of nuclear weapons stockpiles.

D. To Reduce Strategic Nuclear Weapons Delivery Vehicles

(a) Strategic nuclear weapons delivery vehicles in specified categories and agreed types of weapons designed to counter such vehicles shall be reduced to agreed levels by equitable and balanced steps. The reduction shall be accomplished in each step by transfers to depots supervised by the IDO of vehicles that are in excess of levels agreed upon for each step. At specified periods during the Stage I reduction process, the vehicles that have been placed under supervision of the IDO shall be destroyed or converted to peaceful uses.

(b) Production of agreed categories of strategic nuclear weapons delivery vehicles and agreed types of weapons designed to counter such vehicles shall be discontinued or limited.

(c) Testing of agreed categories of strategic nuclear weapons delivery vehicles and agreed types of weapons designed to counter such vehicles shall be limited or halted.

E. To Promote the Peaceful Use of Outer Space

(a) The placing into orbit or stationing in outer space of weapons capable of producing mass destruction shall be prohibited.

(b) States shall give advance notification to participating states and to the IDO of launchings of space vehicles and missiles, together with the track of the vehicle.

F. To Reduce the Risks of War by Accident, Miscalculation, and Surprise Attack

(a) States shall give advance notification to the participating states and to the IDO of major military movements and maneuvers, on a scale as may be agreed, which might give rise to misinterpretation or cause alarm and induce countermeasures. The notification shall include the geographic areas to be used and the nature, scale and time span of the event.

(b) There shall be established observation posts at such locations as major ports, railway centers, motor highways, and air bases to report on concentrations and movements of military forces.

(c) There shall also be established such additional inspection arrangements to reduce the danger of surprise attack as may be agreed.

(d) An international commission shall be established immediately within the IDO to examine and make recommendations on the possibility of further measures to reduce the risks of nuclear war by accident, miscalculation, or failure of communication.

G. To Keep the Peace

(a) States shall reaffirm their obligation under the U.N. Charter to refrain from the threat or use of any type of armed force – including nuclear, conventional, or CBR – contrary to the principles of the U.N. Charter.

(b) States shall agree to refrain from indirect aggression and subversion against any country.

(c) States shall use all appropriate processes for the peaceful settlement of disputes and shall seek within the United

Exceptional Profile of Courage

Nations further arrangements for the peaceful settlement of international disputes and for the codification and progressive development of international law.

(d) States shall develop arrangements in Stage I for the establishment in Stage II of an U.N. Peace Force.

(e) An U.N. peace observation group shall be staffed with a standing cadre of observers who could be dispatched to investigate any situation, which might constitute a threat to or breach of the peace.

STAGE II
A. International Disarmament Organization
The powers and responsibilities of the IDO shall be progressively enlarged in order to give it the capabilities to verify the measures undertaken in Stage II.

B. To Further Reduce Armed Forces and Armaments

(a) Levels of forces for the U.S., U.S.S.R., and other militarily significant states shall be further reduced by substantial amounts to agreed levels in equitable and balanced steps.

(b) Levels of armaments of prescribed types shall be further reduced by equitable and balanced steps. The reduction shall be accomplished by transfers of armaments to depots supervised by the IDO. When, at specified periods during the Stage II reduction process, the parties have agreed that the armaments and armed forces are at prescribed levels, the armaments in depots shall be destroyed or converted to peaceful uses.

(c) There shall be further agreed restrictions on the production of armaments.

(d) Agreed military bases and facilities wherever they are located shall be dismantled or converted to peaceful uses.

(e) Depending upon the findings of the Experts Commission on CBR weapons, the production of CBR weapons shall be halted, existing stocks progressively reduced, and the resulting excess quantities destroyed or converted to peaceful uses.

C. To Further Reduce the Nuclear Threat
Stocks of nuclear weapons shall be progressively reduced to the minimum levels, which can be agreed upon as a result of the findings of the Nuclear Experts Commission; the resulting excess of fissionable material shall be transferred to peaceful purposes.

D. To Further Reduce Strategic Nuclear Weapons Delivery Vehicles
Further reductions in the stocks of strategic nuclear weapons delivery vehicles and agreed type of weapons designed to counter such vehicles shall be carried out in accordance with the procedure outlined in Stage I.

E. To Keep the Peace
During Stage II, states shall develop further the peace-keeping processes of the United Nations, to the end that the United Nations can effectively in Stage III deter or suppress any threat or use of force in violation of the purposes and principles of the United Nations:

(a) States shall agree upon strengthening the structure, authority, and operation of the United Nations so as to assure that the United Nations will be able effectively to protect states against threats to or breaches of the peace.

(b) The U.N. Peace Force shall be established and progressively strengthened.

(c) States shall also agree upon further improvements and developments in rules of international conduct and in processes for peaceful settlement of disputes and differences.

STAGE III
By the time Stage II has been completed, the confidence produced through a verified disarmament program, the acceptance of rules of peaceful international behavior, and the development of strengthened international peace-keeping processes within the framework of the U.N. should have reached a point where the states of the world can move forward to Stage III. In Stage III progressive controlled disarmament and continuously develop-

ing principles and procedures of international law would proceed to a point where no state would have the military power to challenge the progressively strengthened U.N. Peace Force and all international disputes would be settled according to the agreed principles of international conduct.

The progressive steps to be taken during the final phase of the disarmament program would be directed toward the attainment of a world in which:

(a) States would retain only those forces, non-nuclear armaments, and establishments required for the purpose of maintaining internal order; they would also support and provide agreed manpower for a U.N. Peace Force.

(b) The U.N. Peace Force, equipped with agreed types and quantities of armaments, would be fully functioning.

(c) The manufacture of armaments would be prohibited except for those of agreed types and quantities to be used by the U.N. Peace Force and those required to maintain internal order. All other armaments would be destroyed or converted to peaceful purposes.

(d) The peace-keeping capabilities of the United Nations would be sufficiently strong and the obligations of all states under such arrangements sufficiently far-reaching as to assure peace and the just settlement of differences in a disarmed world.

Chapter 12
Review of "Arms Control and Disarmament Act" Public Law 87-297

The 87th Congress, H. R. 9118, on September 26, 1961, enacted Public Law 87-297 identified as "Arms Control and Disarmament Act."

To begin we provide an analysis of a number of its points, so that as you next read the Act, it will have more significance. Following the analysis, the Act is included for your review and information.

The following statements and information regarding Public Law 87-297 were researched and written by Bernadine Smith, Director 2nd Amendment Committee, a private organization in California.

Public Law 87-297 is unconstitutional because it violates one of the major principles for which the Constitution was established: The common defense. In order to be sovereign, the nation must maintain its own army. It cannot transfer its armed forces on a permanent basis to a foreign power – which is a requirement of Public Law 87-297 – and still expect to retain its independence.

Public Law 87-297 seeks World Law to be imposed, which will supersede and destroy the sovereignty of the United States. The court system we are accustomed to, the rights to which we know we are entitled, can be redefined by a World Court.

Exceptional Profile of Courage

Public Law 87-297 can leave us unprotected against invasion. It is also the basis for passage of the Open Skies Treaty 3-24-92, which allows foreign aircraft aerial observation with free access over U.S. air space.

Public Law 87-297 allows the admittance of acknowledged enemies of our nation to become resident inspectors and to monitor into our most key and secret military installations to insure that once the United States reaches the point of "general and complete disarmament" that it has no chance to re-arm the nation.

Public Law 87-297 in compliance with documented policies of the U.S. State Department weakens the nation by dismantling its military bases and causes the destruction of existing weapons, which are superior to those of the enemies of our nation.

Public Law 87-297 sacrifices the independence of our civilian law enforcement systems by promoting their replacement with a unified national policing system under the approval of a foreign power.

Public Law 87-297 in Title I Definitions. Section 3 of the Act defines the meaning of disarmament as follows:
Section 3. As used in this Act –
(a) The terms "arms control" and "disarmament" mean the identification, verification, inspection, limitation, control, reduction, or elimination of armed forces and armaments of all kinds under international agreement including the necessary steps taken under such an agreement to establish an effective system of international control, or to create and strengthen international organizations for the maintenance of peace.

Public Law 87-297 in Title III Functions. Section 31 regarding the authority of the Director calls for the destruction of among others, our conventional as well as other weapons and states:
(a) The detection, identification, inspection, monitoring, limitation, reduction, control, and elimination of armed forces

and armaments, including thermonuclear, nuclear, missile, conventional, bacteriological, chemical, and radiological weapons; (This is why so many privately-owned firearms are being condemned as "military and assault weapons.")

(d) the control, reduction, and elimination of armed forces and armaments in space, in areas on and beneath the earth's surface, and in underwater regions;

(f) the training of scientists, technicians, and other personnel for manning the control systems which may be created by international arms control and disarmament agreements;

Public Law 87-297 allows the United States to be under an international "peace-keeping Force." Title I Section 3 (a) it is also responsible for the Soviet-American Police Exchange Program.

Public Law 87-297 confers upon the President the power to make treaties with foreign powers which disarm or reduce or limit the Armed Forces or armaments of the United States, to close our military bases. Title III Section 33

Public Law 87-297 is the underlying reason why so many public officials are passing laws in violation of the inherent rights of the people in the Second Amendment of the Bill of Rights and are moving to get all the firearms away from the people for purposes of "ultimate world disarmament" as called for in Title I Section 2.

The strategically drafted Section 2573 of Title 22 (added in 1963 to stop the public outcry against this 1961 disarmament law) has been superseded and rendered meaningless as it states: "Nothing contained in this chapter shall be construed to authorize any policy...which would interfere with, restrict, or prohibit the acquisition, possession or use of firearms by an individual for the lawful purpose of personal defense, sport, recreation, education or training" because in the same section it also states:

Exceptional Profile of Courage

"Provided, however, That no action shall be taken under this or any other law that will obligate the United States to disarm or to reduce or to limit the Armed Forces or armaments of the United States, except pursuant to the treaty making power of the President under the Constitution or unless authorized by further affirmative legislation by the Congress of the United States."

Which now has happened since President Clinton signed treaties and the Congress is writing laws to do away with citizen-owned firearms.

Some legal scholars believe that unless we call for the repeal of Public Law 87-297 and its Amendments, your guns will be past history.

Public Law 87-297 is part of a disarmament plan, under John F. Kennedy's watchful eye, to turn over the military forces of the United States of America to the United Nations jurisdictional authority. This Public Law is cleverly conceived by the proponents of a one-world government also known as the "New World Order" to take from the people of American the liberty that we so love, its ability to defend itself against government tyranny. The main reason our founding fathers gave us the second Amendment, "The right of the people to keep and bear arms, shall not be infringed," *was to defend ourselves*.

In June, 2001 the United Nations Conference was held on the Illicit Trade in Small Arms and Light Weapons. The purpose of this conference was to advance the development of an international treaty to control the availability of small arms and light weapons in warfare.

On that occasion, the United Nations General Assembly approved a gun control treaty that calls on all nations "to prevent, combat and eradicate the illicit manufacturing of an trafficking in firearms, their parts and components, and ammunition."

The treaty is supposed to make it much easier to crack down on illegal gun trafficking by helping authorities trace the global movement of all new weapons. When signed and ratified by 40

countries, it then becomes international law. The signing runs between July 1 to Dec. 12, 2002.
- Every new firearm would be marked with a serial number and the place of manufacture.
- Each country would be required to keep records on all guns, parts and ammunition made within their country for a period of ten years.
- Each country is urged to pass laws making the illicit manufacture and sale of firearms a criminal offense.

IANSA is an organization called International Action Network on Small Arms. This international network of over 340 organizations from 71 countries works to prevent proliferation and misuse of small arms and light weapons.

Chapter 13
Text of – "Arms Control and Disarmament Act" Public Law 87-297

TITLE I – SHORT TITLE, PURPOSE, AND DEFINITIONS

SHORT TITLE **Section 1.** This Act may be cited as the "Arms Control and Disarmament Act."

PURPOSE

Section 2. An ultimate goal of the United States is a world which is free from the scourge of war and the dangers and burdens of armaments; in which the use of force has been subordinated to the rule of law; and in which international adjustments to a changing world are achieved peacefully. It is the purpose of this Act to provide impetus toward this goal by creating a new agency of peace to deal with the problem of reduction and control of armaments looking toward ultimate world disarmament.

Arms control and disarmament policy, being an important aspect of foreign policy, must be consistent with national security policy as a whole. The formulation and implementation of United States arms control and disarmament policy in a manner which will promote the national security can best be insured by a central organization charged by statute with primary responsibility for this field. This organization must have such a position within the Government that it can provide the President, the Secretary of State, other officials of the executive branch, and the

Congress with recommendations concerning United States arms control and disarmament policy, and can assess the effect of these recommendations upon our foreign policies, our national security policies, and our economy.

This organization must have the capacity to provide the essential scientific, economic, political, military, psychological, and technological information upon which realistic arms control and disarmament policy must be based. It must be able to carry out the following primary functions:

(a) The conduct, support, and coordination of research for arms control and disarmament policy formulation;

(b) The preparation for and management of United States participation in international negotiations in the arms control and disarmament field;

(c) The dissemination and coordination of public information concerning arms control and disarmament; and

(d) The preparation for, operation of, or as appropriate, direction of United States participation in such control systems as may become part of United States arms control and disarmament activities.

DEFINITIONS

Section 3. As used in this Act –

(a) The terms "arms control" and "disarmament" mean the identification, verification, inspection, limitation, control, reduction, or elimination, of armed forces and armaments of all kinds under international agreement including the necessary steps taken under such an agreement to establish an effective system of international control, or to create and strengthen international organizations for the maintenance of peace.

(b) The term "Government agency" means any executive department, commission, agency, independent establishment, corporation wholly or partly owned by the United States which is an instrumentality of the United States, or any board, bureau, division, service, office officer, authority, administration, or other establishment in the executive branch of Government.

(c) The term "Agency" means the United States Arms Control and Disarmament Agency.

TITLE II – ORGANIZATION

UNITED STATES ARMS CONTROL AND DISARMAMENT AGENCY

Section 21. There is hereby established an agency to be known as the "United States Arms Control and Disarmament Agency."

DIRECTOR

Section 22. The Agency shall be headed by a Director, who shall serve as the principal adviser to the Secretary of State and the President on arms control and disarmament matters. In carrying out his duties under this Act the Director shall, under the direction of the Secretary of State, have primary responsibility within the Government for arms control and disarmament matters, as defined in this Act. He shall be appointed by the President, by and with the advice and consent of the Senate. He shall receive compensation at the rate of $22,500 per annum.

DEPUTY DIRECTOR

Section 23. A Deputy Director of the Agency shall be appointed by the President, by and with the advice and consent of the Senate. He shall receive compensation at the rate of $21,500 per annum. The Deputy Director shall perform such duties and exercise such powers as the Director may prescribe. He shall act for, and exercise the powers of, the Director during his absence or disability or during a vacancy in said office.

ASSISTANT DIRECTORS

Section 24. Not to exceed four Assistant Directors may be appointed by the President, by and with the advice and consent of the Senate. They shall receive compensation at the rate of $20,000 per annum. They shall perform such duties and exercise such powers as the Director may prescribe.

BUREAUS, OFFICES, AND DIVISIONS

Section 25. The Director, under the direction of the Secretary of State, may establish within the Agency such bureaus, offices, and divisions as he may determine to be necessary to discharge his responsibilities under this Act, including, but not limited to, an Office of the General Counsel.

GENERAL ADVISORY COMMITTEE

Section 26. The President, by and with the advice and consent of the Senate, may appoint a General Advisory Committee of not to exceed fifteen members to advise the Director on arms control and disarmament policy and activities. The President shall designate one of the members as Chairman. The members of the committee may receive the compensation and reimbursement for expenses specified for consultants by section 41 (d) of this Act. The Committee shall meet at least twice each year. It shall from time to time advise the President, the Secretary of State, and the Disarmament Director respecting matters affecting arms control, disarmament, and world peace.

TITLE III – FUNCTIONS

RESEARCH

Section 31. The Director is authorized and directed to exercise his powers in such manner as to insure the acquisition of a fund of theoretical and practical knowledge concerning disarmament. To this end, the Director is authorized and directed, under the direction of the President, (1) to insure the conduct of research, development, and other studies in the field of arms control and disarmament; (2) to make arrangements (including contracts, agreement, and grants) for the conduct of research, development, and other studies in the field of arms control and disarmament by private or public institutions or persons; and (3) to coordinate the research, development, and other studies conducted in the field of arms control and disarmament by or for other Government agencies in accordance with procedures established under section 35 of this Act. In carrying out his responsibilities under this Act, the Director shall, to the maximum extent feasible, make full use of available facilities, Government and private. The authority of the Director with respect to research, development, and other studies shall be limited to participation in the following insofar as they relate to arms control and disarmament:

(a) the detection, identification, inspection, monitoring, limitation, reduction, control, and elimination of armed forces and armaments, including thermonuclear, nuclear, missile, conventional, bacteriological, chemical, and radiological weapons;

(b) the techniques and systems of detecting, identifying, inspecting, and monitoring of tests of nuclear, thermonuclear, and other weapons;

(c) the analysis of national budgets, levels of industrial production, and economic indicators to determine the amounts spent by various countries for armaments;

(d) the control, reduction, and elimination of armed forces and armaments in space, in areas on and beneath the earth's surface, and in underwater regions;

(e) the structure and operation of international control and other organizations useful for arms control and disarmament;

(f) the training of scientists, technicians, and other personnel for manning the control systems which may be created by international arms control and disarmament agreements;

(g) the reduction and elimination of the danger of war resulting from accident, miscalculation, or possible surprise attack, including (but not limited to) improvements in the methods of communications between nations;

(h) the economic and political consequences of arms control and disarmament, including the problems of readjustment arising in industry and the reallocation of national resources;

(i) the arms control and disarmament implications of foreign and national security policies of the United States with a view to a better understanding of the significance of such policies for the achievement of arms control and disarmament;

(j) the national security and foreign policy implications of arms control and disarmament proposals with a view to a better understanding of the effect of such proposals upon national security and foreign policy;

(k) methods for the maintenance of peace and security during different stages of arms control and disarmament;

(l) the scientific, economic, political, legal, social, psychological, military, and technological factors related to the prevention of war with a view to a better understanding of how the basic structure of a lasting peace may be established;

(m) such related problems as the Director may determine to be in need of research, development, or study in order to carry out the provision of this Act.

PATENTS

Section 32. All research within the United States contracted for, sponsored, cosponsored, or authorized under authority of this Act, shall be provided for in such manner that all information as to uses, products, processes, patents, and other developments resulting from such developed by Government expenditure will with such exceptions and limitations, if any, as the Director may find to be necessary in the public interest, be available to the general public. This subsection shall not be so construed as to deprive the owner of any background patent relating thereto of such rights as he may have thereunder.

POLICY FORMULATION

Section 33. The Director is authorized and directed to prepare for the President, the Secretary of State, and the heads of such other Government agencies, as the President may determine, recommendations concerning United States arms control and disarmament policy: Provided however, That no action shall be taken under this or any other law that will obligate the United States to disarm or to reduce or to limit the Armed Forces or armaments of the United States, except pursuant to the treaty making power of the President under the Constitution or unless authorized by further affirmative legislation by the Congress of the United States.

NEGOTIATIONS AND RELATED FUNCTIONS

Section 34. Under the direction of the Secretary of State –

(a) the Director, for the purpose of conducting negotiations concerning arms control and disarmament or for the purpose of exercising any other authority given him by this Act, may (1) consult and communicate with or direct the consultation and communication with representatives of other nations or of international organizations and (2) communicate in the name of the Secretary with diplomatic representatives of the United States in this country and abroad.

(b) the Director shall perform functions pursuant to section 2 (c) of Reorganization Plan 8 of 1953 with respect to providing to the United States Information Agency official United States positions and policy on arms control and disarmament matters for dissemination abroad.

(c) the Director is authorized (1) to formulate plans and make preparations for the establishment, operation, and funding of inspection and control systems which may become part of the United States arms control and disarmament activities, and (2) as authorized by law, to put into effect, direct, or otherwise assume United States responsibility for such systems.

COORDINATION

Section 35. The President is authorized to establish procedures to (1) assure cooperation, consultation, and a continuing exchange of information between the Agency and the Department of Defense, the Atomic Energy Commission, the National Aeronautics and Space Administration and other affected Government agencies, in all significant aspects of United States arms control and disarmament policy and related matters, including current and prospective policies, plans, and programs, (2) resolve differences of opinion between the Director and such other agencies which cannot be resolved through consultation, and (3) provide for presentation to the president of recommendations of the Director with respect to such differences, when such differences involve major matters of policy and cannot be resolved through consultation.

TITLE IV – GENERAL PROVISIONS

GENERAL AUTHORITY

Section 41. In the performance of his functions, the Director is authorized to –

(a) utilize or employ the services, personnel, equipment, or facilities of any other Government agency, with the consent of the agency concerned, to perform such functions on behalf of the Agency as may appear desirable. It is the intent of this section that the Director rely upon the Department of State for general administrative services in the United States and abroad to the extent agreed upon between the Secretary of State and the Director. Any Government agency is authorized, notwithstanding any other provision of law, to transfer to or to receive from the Director, without reimbursement, supplies and equipment other than administrative supplies or equipment. Transfer or receipt of excess property shall be in accordance with the provisions of the Federal Property and Administrative Services Act of 1949, as amended;

(b) appoint officers and employees, including attorneys, for the Agency in accordance with the civil service laws and fix their compensation in accordance with the Classification Act of 1949, as amended:

(c) enter into agreements with other Government agencies, including the military departments through the Secretary of Defense under which officers or employees of such agencies may be detailed to the Agency for the performance of service pursuant to this Act without prejudice to the status or advancement of such officers or employees within their own agencies;

(d) procure services of experts and consultants or organizations thereof, including stenographic reporting services, as authorized by section 15 of the Act of August 2, 1946 (5 U. S. C. 55a), at rates not to exceed $100 per diem for individuals, and to pay in connection therewith travel expenses of individuals, including transportation and per diem in lieu of subsistence while away from their homes or regular places of business, as authorized by section 5 of said Act, as amended (5 U.S.C. 73b-2) Provided, That no such individual shall be employed for more than one hundred days in any fiscal year unless the President certifies that employment of such individual in excess of such number of days is necessary in the national interest: And provided further, That such contracts may be renewed annually;

(e) employ individuals of outstanding ability without compensation in accordance with the provisions of section 710(b) of the Defense Production Act of 1950, as amended (50 U.S.C. App. 2160), and regulations issued thereunder;

(f) establish advisory boards to advise with and make recommendations to the Director on United States arms control and disarmament policy and activities. The members of such boards may receive the compensation and reimbursement for expenses specified for consultants by section 41 (d) of this Act;

(g) delegate, as appropriate, to the Deputy Director or other officers of the Agency, any authority conferred upon the Director by the provisions of this Act; and

(h) make, promulgate, issue, rescind, and amend such rules and regulations as may be necessary or desirable to the exercise of any authority conferred upon the Director by the provisions of this Act.

FOREIGN SERVICE RESERVE AND STAFF OFFICERS

Section 42. The Secretary of State may authorize the Director to exercise, with respect to Foreign Service Reserve officers and Foreign Service Staff officers and employees appointed or employed for the Agency, the following authority; (1) The authority available to the Secretary of State under the Foreign Service Act of 1946, as amended, (2) the authority available to the Secretary under any other provision of law pertaining specifically, or generally applicable, to such officers or employees, and (3) the authority of the Board of Foreign Service pursuant to the Foreign Service Act of 1946, as amended.

CONTRACTS OR EXPENDITURES

Section 43. The President may, in advance, exempt actions of the Director from the provisions of law relating to contracts or expenditures of Government funds whenever he determines that such action is essential in the interest of United States arms control and disarmament and security policy.

CONFLICT OF INTEREST AND DUAL COMPENSATION LAWS

Section 44. The members of the General Advisory Committee created by section 26 of this Act, and the members of the advisory boards, the consultants, and the individuals of outstanding ability employed without compensation, all of which are provided in section 41 of this Act, may serve as such without regard to the provisions of section 281, 283, 284 or 1914 of title 18 of the United States Code, or of section 190 of the Revised Statutes (5 U.S. C. 99), or of any other Federal law imposing restrictions, requirements, or penalties in relation to the employment of individuals, the performance of services, or the payment or receipt of compensation in connection with any claim, proceeding, or matter involving the United States Government, except insofar as such provisions of law may prohibit any such individual from receiving compensation from a source other than a nonprofit educational institution in respect of any particular matter in which the Agency is directly interested. Nor shall such service be considered as employment or holding of office or position bringing such individual within the provisions of section 13 of the Civil Service Retirement Act (5 U.S. C. 2263), section 212 of the Act of June 30, 1932, as amended (5 U.S. C. 59a), or any other Federal law limiting the re-employment of retired officers or employees or governing the simultaneous receipt of compensation and retired pay or annuities.

SECURITY REQUIREMENTS

Section 45.

(a) The Director shall establish such security and loyalty requirements, restrictions, and safeguards as he deems necessary in the interest of the national security and to carry out the provisions of this Act. The Director shall arrange with the Civil Service Commission for the conduct of full-field background security and loyalty investigations of all the Agency's officers, employees, consultants, persons detailed from other Government agencies, members of its General Advisory Committee, advisory boards, contractors and subcontractors, and their officers and employees, actual or prospective. In the event the investigation discloses information indicating that the person investigated may be or may become a security risk, or may be of doubtful loyalty, the report of the investigation shall be turned over to the Federal Bureau of Investigation for a full-field investigation. The final results of all such investigations shall be turned over to the Director for final determination. No person shall be permitted to enter on duty as such an officer, employee, consultant, or member of advisory committee or board, or pursuant to any such detail, and no contractor or subcontractor, or officer or employee thereof shall be permitted to have access to any classified information, until he shall have been investigated in accordance with this subsection and the report of such investigations made to the Director, and the Director shall have determined that such person is not a security risk or of doubtful loyalty. Standards applicable with respect to the security clearance of persons within any category referred to in this subsection shall not be less stringent, and the investigation of such persons for such purposes shall not be less intensive or complete, than in the case of such clearance of persons in a corresponding category under the security procedures of the Government agency or agencies having the highest security restrictions with respect to persons in such category.

(b) The Atomic Energy Commission may authorize any of its employees, or employees of any contractor, prospective contractor, licensee, or prospective licensee of the Atomic Energy Commission or any other person authorized to have access to Restricted Data by the Atomic Energy Commission under section 2165 of title 42, to permit the Director or any officer, employee, consultant, person detailed from other Government agencies, member of the General Advisory Committee or of an advisory board established pursuant to section 41 (f), contractor, subcontractor, prospective contractor, or prospective subcontractor, or officer or employee of such contractor, subcontractor, prospective contractor, or prospective subcontractor, to have access to Restricted Data which is required in the performance of his duties and so certified by the Director, but only if (1) the Atomic Energy Commission has determined, in accordance with the established personnel security procedures and standards of the Commission, that permitting such individual to have access to such Restricted Data will not endanger the common defense and security, and (2) the Atomic Energy Commission finds that the established personnel and other security procedures and standards of the Agency are adequate and in reasonable conformity to the standards established by the Atomic Energy Commission under section 2165 of title 42, including those for interim clearance in subsection (b) thereof. Any individual granted access to such Restricted Data pursuant to this subsection may exchange such data with any individual who (A) is an officer or employee of the Department of Defense, or any department or agency thereof, or a member of the Armed Forces, or an officer or employee of the National Aeronautics and Space Administration, or a contractor or subcontractor of any such department, agency, or armed forces, or an officer or employee of any such contractor or subcontractor, and (B) has been authorized to have access to Restricted Data under the provisions of section 2163 or 2455 of title 42.

COMPTROLLER GENERAL AUDIT

Section 46. No moneys appropriated for the purpose of this Act shall be available for payment under any contract with the Director, negotiated without advertising, except contracts with any foreign government, international organization or any agency thereof, unless such contract includes a clause to the effect that the Comptroller General of the United States or any of his duly authorized representatives shall, until the expiration of three years after final payment, have access to and the right to examine any directly pertinent books, documents, papers, and records of the contractor or any of his subcontractors engaged in the performance of, and involving transactions related to such contracts or subcontracts: Provided, however, That no moneys so appropriated shall

Exceptional Profile of Courage

be available for payment under such contract which includes any provisions precluding an audit by the General Accounting Office of any transaction under such contract: And provided further, That nothing in this section shall preclude the earlier disposal of contractor and subcontractor records in accordance with records disposal schedules agreed upon between the Director and the General Accounting Office.

TRANSFER OF ACTIVITIES AND FACILITIES TO AGENCY

Section 47.

(a) The United States Disarmament Administration, together with its records, property, personnel, and funds, is hereby transferred to the Agency. The appropriations and unexpended balances of appropriations transferred pursuant to this subsection shall be available for expenditure for any and all objects of expenditure authorized by this Act, without regard to the requirements of apportionment under section 665 of title 31.

(b) The President, by Executive order, may transfer to the Director any activities or facilities of any Government agency which relate primarily to arms control and disarmament. In connection with any such transfer, the President may under this section or other applicable authority, provide for appropriate transfers of records, property, civilian personnel, and funds. No transfer shall be made under this subsection until (1) a full and complete report concerning the nature and effect of such proposed transfer has been transmitted by the President to the Congress, and (2) the first period of sixty calendar days of regular session of the Congress following the date of receipt of such report by the Congress has expired without adoption by either House of the Congress of a resolution stating that such House does not favor such transfer. The procedures prescribed in title II of the Reorganization Act of 1949 shall apply to any such resolution.

USE OF FUNDS

Section 48. Appropriations made to the Director for the purposes of this Act, and transfers of funds to him by other Government agencies for such purposes, shall be available to him to exercise any authority granted him by this Act, including, without limitation, expenses of printing and binding without regard to the provisions of section 11 of the Act of March 1, 1919 (44 U.S. C. 111); purchase or hire of one passenger motor vehicle for the official use of the Director without regard to the limitations contained in section 78 (c) of title 5 of the United States Code; entertainment and official courtesies to the extent authorized by appropriation; expenditures for training and study; expenditures in connection with participation in international conferences for the purposes of this Act; and expenses in connection with travel of personnel outside the United States, including transportation expenses of dependents, household goods, and personal effects and expenses authorized by the Foreign Service Act of 1946, as amended, not otherwise provided for.

APPROPRIATION

Section 49.
(a) There are hereby authorized to be appropriated not to exceed $10,000,000 to remain available until expended, to carry out the purposes of this Act.

(b) Funds appropriated pursuant to this section may be allocated or transferred to any agency for carrying out the purposes of this Act. Such funds shall be available for obligation and expenditure in accordance with authority granted in this Act, or under authority governing the activities of the agencies to which such funds are allocated or transferred.

REPORT TO CONGRESS

Section 50. The Director shall submit to the President, for transmittal to the Congress, not later than January 31 of each year, a report concerning activities of the Agency.

Approved September 26, 1961, 12:45 p.m.

Chapter 14
The Solution
HR 1146 – The American Sovereignty Restoration Act of 2001

Congressman Ron Paul (R-Texas) reintroduced HR 1146, "American Sovereignty Restoration Act of 2001" on March 21, 2001. This bill is the same in wording as the bill introduced in the 106th Congress. The two cosponsors are: Bob Stump (R-Ariz) and Richard Pombo (R-Calif).

This Constitutional Analysis by Herbert W. Titus, a Legal Advisor to Congressman Paul gives us the insight in understanding HR 1146 and its true intent.

The Liberty Committee has given me permission to include the Constitutional Analysis in its entirety as follows:

I. Summary
II. Introduction
III. The Charter of the United Nations is Illegitimate, Having Never Been Lawfully Ratified
IV. The Charter of the United Nations Unlawfully Delegates Congressional and Presidential War Powers
V. The United Nations General Assembly has no Lawful Power to Require the United States to Pay Dues to the United Nations
VI. The Charter of the United Nations Unconstitutionally Usurps Power Reserved to the States by the Tenth Amendment

VII.	Conclusion: HR 1146 – The American Sovereignty Restoration Act of 2001 is the Only Viable Solution to the Continued Abuses of the United Nations

I. Summary

The Charter of the United Nations is neither politically nor legally binding upon the United States of America or the American people.

The Charter of the United Nations is commonly assumed to be a treaty. It is not. Instead, the Charter of the United Nations is a constitution. As such, it is illegitimate, having created a supranational government, deriving its powers not from the consent of the governed (the people of the United States and peoples of other member nations) but from the consent of the peoples' government officials who have no authority to bind either the American people nor any other nation's people to any terms of the Charter of the United Nations.

Even if the Charter of the United Nations were a properly-ratified treaty, it would still be constitutionally illegitimate and void because it transgresses the Constitution of the United States of America in three major respects:
1. It unconstitutionally delegates to the United Nations the U.S. Congress' legislative power to initiate war and the U.S. President's executive power to conduct war;
2. It unconstitutionally transfers to the United Nations General Assembly the United States House of Representatives' exclusive power to originate revenue-raising measures; and,
3. It unconstitutionally robs the 50 American States of powers reserved to them by the Tenth Amendment of the Constitution of the United States of America.

HR 1146 – The American Sovereignty Restoration Act of 2001 is the only viable solution to the continued abuses of the United Nations. The U.S. Congress can remedy its earlier unconstitutional action of embracing the Charter of the United Nations by enacting HR 1146. The U.S. Congress, by passing HR 1146, and

Exceptional Profile of Courage

the U.S. President by signing HR 1146, will heed the counsel of our first President, George Washington, when he advised his countrymen to "steer clear of permanent alliances with any portion of the foreign world," lest the Nation's security and liberties be compromised by endless and overriding international commitments.

II Introduction

Over half a century has transpired since the United States of America became a member of the United Nations. Purporting to act pursuant to the treaty power (Article II, Section 2) of the Constitution of the United States of America (Constitution), the President of the United States signed and the United States Senate ratified the Charter of the United Nations. Yet, as Edwin S. Corwin's classic study of <u>The President: Office and Powers,</u> has observed, "the debate in government circles over the United Nations' charter scarcely touched on the question of the constitutional power of the United States to enter such an arrangement..."E. Corwin, <u>The President 248 (5th Rev. ed. 1984)</u>. Instead, the only questions addressed concerned the respective roles that the President and Congress would assume upon the implementation of that charter.

On the one hand, some proposed that once the charter of the United Nations was ratified, the President of the United States would act independently of Congress pursuant to his executive prerogative to conduct the foreign affairs of the Nation. Others insisted, however, that Congress play the major role of defining U.S. foreign policy, especially because that policy implicated the power to declare war, a subject expressly reserved to Congress by Article I, Section 8 of the Constitution of the United States of America.

At first, it appeared that Congress would take control of America's participation in the United Nations. By the enactment of the United Nations Participation Act on December 20, 1945, Congress laid down several rules by which America's participation would be governed.

Among those rules was the requirement that before the President of the United States could deploy United States armed forces in service of the United Nations, he was required to submit to Congress for its specific approval "the numbers and types of armed forces, their degree of readiness and general location, and the nature of the facilities and assistance, including rights of passage, to be made available to the United Nations Security Council on its call for the purpose of maintaining international peace and security."

As Corwin has pointed out, "the controlling theory of the act is that American participation in United Nations shall rest on the principle of department collaboration, and not on an exclusive presidential prerogative in the diplomatic field." Id. at 251

> Since the passage of the United Nations Participation Act, however, congressional control of presidential foreign policy initiatives in cooperation with the United Nations has been more theoretical than real.

Presidents from Truman to Clinton have again and again presented Congress with military *faits accomplis*, thereby forcing Congress' hand to support United States troops or risk the accusation of having put the Nation's servicemen and servicewomen in unnecessary danger.

Instead of seeking congressional approval of the use of United States armed forces in service of the United Nations, presidents from Truman to Clinton have used the United Nations Security Council as a substitute for congressional authorization of the deployment of United States armed forces in that service.

This erosion of congressional power, and hence United States sovereignty, has not been accidental. The seeds were planted from the beginning, both in the text of the Charter of the United Nations and in the vision of its most ardent supporters.

Article 24 of the Charter of the United Nations proclaimed that, as necessary prerequisite for "prompt and effective action," the members of the United Nations "confer (red) on the Security Council primary responsibility for the maintenance of international peace and security," agreeing "that in carrying out its duties under this responsibility the Security Council acts on their behalf."

Exceptional Profile of Courage

With such expansive language as this, it is not surprising that, even before the charter was ratified, President Franklin Delano Roosevelt expressed hope that some day "the lion's share" of "the direction of American foreign policy" would pass gradually to the United Nations Security Council. Id., at 249-50

This transfer of power from Congress to the United Nations has not, however, been limited to the power to make war. Increasingly, presidents are using the United Nations not only to implement foreign policy in pursuit of international peace, but also domestic policy in pursuit of international, environmental, economic, education, social welfare, and human rights policies, both in derogation of the legislative prerogatives of Congress and of the 50 State legislatures, and further, in derogation of the rights of the American people to constitute their own civil order. As Cornell University government professor Jeremy Rabkin has observed:

> Although the Charter specifies (Art. 2, Para. 7) that none of its provisions "shall authorize the United Nations to intervene in matters which are essentially within the domestic jurisdiction of any state," nothing has ever been found so "essentially domestic" as to exclude UN intrusions. J. Rabkin, Why Sovereignty Matters 31 (AEI Press, Washington, D.C.: 1998).

The release in July 2000 of the United Nations Human Development Report 2000 provides unmistakable evidence of the universality of the United Nation's jurisdictional claims. Boldly proclaiming that "global integration is...eroding national borders," the report calls for the implementation and, if necessary, the imposition of global standards of economic and social justice by international agencies and tribunals. In a "special contribution" endorsing this call for the internationalization of domestic policymaking, United Nations Secretary General Kofi Annan wrote:

> At the dawn of the 21st century, the United Nations has become more central to the lives of more people than ever...Above all...we have committed ourselves to the idea that no individual...shall have his or her human rights abused or ignored. This idea is enshrined in the

Charter of the United Nations...The United Nations' achievements in the area of human rights over the last 50 years are rooted in the universal acceptance of those rights enumerated in the Universal Declaration (of Rights)...Emerging slowly, but I believe, surely, is an international norm,,,that must and will take precedence over concerns of state sovereignty. UN <u>Human Development Report 2000</u> 31 (July 2000) (Emphasis added.)
Although such a wholesale transfer of United States sovereignty to the United Nations as envisioned by Secretary General Kofi Annan, has not yet come to pass, it will–unless Congress takes action.

To date, Congress has attempted to curb the abuse of power of the United Nations by urging the United Nations to reform itself, threatening the nonpayment of assessments and dues allegedly owed by the United States and thereby cutting off the United Nation's major source of funds. America's problems with the United Nations will not, however, be solved by such reform measures.

The threat posed by the United Nations to the sovereignty of the United States and independence is not that the United Nations is currently plagued by a bloated and irresponsible international bureaucracy. Rather, the threat arises from the United Nation's very existence, the Charter of the United Nations of which – from the beginning – was designed to displace the national charter of the United States of America – the Declaration of Independence and her national covenant – the Constitution of the United States of America.

The American people have not, however, ever approved the Charter of the United Nations which, by its nature, cannot be the supreme law of the land for it was never "made under the Authority of the United States," as required by Article VI of the Constitution of the United States of America.

III. The Charter of the United Nations is Illegitimate, Having Never Been Lawfully Ratified

It is commonly assumed that the Charter of the United Nations is a treaty. It is not. Instead, the Charter of the United Nations is a constitution. As such, it is illegitimate, having created a supranational government, deriving its powers not from the consent of the governed (the people of the United States of America and peoples of other member nations) but from the consent of the peoples' government officials who have no authority to bind either the American people nor any other nation's people to any terms of the Charter of the United Nations.

By definition, a treaty is a contract between or among independent and sovereign nations, obligatory on the signatories only when made by competent governing authorities in accordance with the powers constitutionally conferred upon them. I Kent, Commentaries on American Law 163 (1826); Burdick, The Law of the American Constitution section 34 (1922) Even the United Nations Treaty Collection states that a treaty is (1) a binding instrument creating legal rights and duties (2) concluded by states or international organizations with treaty-making power (3) governed by international law.

By contrast, a charter is a constitution creating a civil government for a unified nation or nations and establishing the authority of that government. Although the United Nations Treaty Collection defines a "charter" as a "constituent treaty," leading international political authorities state that "the use of the word 'Charter' (in reference to the founding document of the United Nations)...emphasizes the constitutional nature of this instrument." Thus, the preamble to the Charter of the United Nations declares "that the Peoples of the United Nations have resolved to combine their efforts to accomplish certain aims by certain means." The Charter of the United Nations: A Commentary 46 (B. Simma, ed.) (Oxford Univ. Press, NY: 1995) (Hereinafter U.S. Charter Commentary)

Consistent with this view, leading international legal authorities declare that the law of the Charter of the United Nations which governs the authority of the United Nations General Assembly and the United Nations Security Council is "similar...to national constitutional law," proclaiming that "because of its status as a constitution for the world community," the Charter of the United

Nations must be construed broadly, making way for "implied powers" to carry out the United Nations' "comprehensive scope of duties, especially the maintenance of international peace and security and its orientation towards international public welfare." Id. at 27

The United Nations Treaty Collection confirms the appropriateness of this "constitutional interpretive" approach to the Charter of the United Nations with its statement that the charter may be traced "back to the Magna Carta (the Great Charter) of 1215," a national constitutional document. As a constitutional document, the Magna Carta not only bound the original signatories, the English barons and the king, but all subsequent English rulers, including Parliament, conferring upon all Englishmen certain rights that five hundred years later were claimed and exercised by the English people who had colonized America.

A charter, then, is a covenant of the people and the civil rulers of a nation in perpetuity. <u>Sources of Our Liberties</u> 1-10 (R. Perry, ed.) (American Bar Foundation: 1978) As Article 1 of Magna Carta, puts it:

> We have granted moreover to all free men of our kingdom for us and our heirs forever all liberties written below, to be had and holden by themselves and their heirs from us and our heirs.

In like manner, the Charter of the United Nations is considered to be a permanent "constitution for the universal society." And consequently, to be construed in accordance with its broad and unchanging ends but in such a way as to meet changing times and changing relations among the nations and peoples of the world. <u>U.N. Charter Commentary</u> at 28-44.

According to the American political and legal tradition and the universal principles of constitution making, a perpetual civil covenant or constitution, obligatory on the people and their rulers throughout the generations, must, first, be proposed in the name of the people and, thereafter, ratified by the people's representatives elected and assembled for the sole purpose of passing on the terms of a proposed covenant. See 4 <u>The Founders' Constitution</u> 647-58 (P. Kurland and R. Lerner, eds.) (Univ. Chicago. Press: 1985).

Thus, the preamble of the Constitution of the United States of America begins with "We the People of the United States: and Article VII provides for ratification by State conventions composed of representatives of the people elected solely for that purpose. <u>Sources of our liberties</u> 408, 416, 418-21 (R. Perry, ed.) (ABA Foundation, Chicago: 1978)

Taking advantage of the universal appeal of the American constitutional tradition, the preamble of the Charter of the United Nations opens with "We the Peoples of the United Nations." But, unlike the Constitution of the United States of America, the Charter of the United Nations does not call for ratification by conventions of the elected representatives of the people of the signatory nations.

Rather, Article 110 of the Charter of the United Nations provides for ratification "by the signatory states in accordance with their respective constitutional processes." Such a ratification process would have been politically and legally appropriate if the charter were a mere treaty. But the Charter of the United Nations is not a treaty; it is a constitution.

First of all, Charter of the United Nations, executed as an agreement in the name of the people, legally and politically displaced previously binding agreements upon the signatory nations.

Article 103 provides that "in the event of a conflict between the obligations of the Members of the United Nations under the present Charter and their obligations under any other international agreement, their obligations under the present Charter shall prevail."

Because the 1787 Constitution of the United States of America would displace the previously adopted Articles of Confederation under which the United States was being governed, the drafters recognized that only if the elected representatives of the people at a constitutional convention ratified the proposed constitution, could it be lawfully adopted as a constitution. Otherwise, the Constitution of the United States of America would be, legally and politically, a treaty which could be altered by any state's legislature as it saw fit. 4 The Founders" Constitution, supra, at 648-52

Second, an agreement made in the name of the people creates a perpetual union, subject to dissolution only upon proof of breach of covenant by the governing authorities whereupon the people are entitled to reconstitute a new government on such terms and for such duration as the people see fit.

By contrast, an agreement made in the name of nations creates only a contractual obligation, subject to change when any signatory nation decides that the obligation is no longer advantageous or suitable. Thus, a treaty may be altered by valid statute enacted by a signatory nation, but a constitution may be altered only by a special amendatory process provided for in that document. Id. at 652

Article V of the Constitution of the United States of America spells out that amendment process, providing two methods for adopting constitutional changes, neither of which requires unanimous consent of the states of the Union. Had the Constitution of the United States of America been a treaty, such unanimous consent would have been required.

Similarly, the Charter of the United Nations may be amended without the unanimous consent of its member states. According to Article 108 of the Charter of the United Nations, amendments may be proposed by a vote of two-thirds of the United Nations General Assembly and may become effective upon ratification by a vote of two-thirds of the members of the United Nations, including all the permanent members of the United Nations Security Council.

According to Article 109 of the Charter of the United Nations, a special conference of members of the United Nations may be called "for the purpose of reviewing the present Charter" and any changes proposed by the conference may "take effect when ratified by two-thirds of the Members of the United Nations including all the permanent members of the Security Council."

Once an amendment to the Charter of the United Nations is adopted then that amendment "shall come into force for all Members of the United Nations," even those nations who did not ratify the amendment, just as an amendment to the Constitution of the United States of America is effective in all of the states, even though the legislature of a state or a convention of a state refused to ratify. Such an amendment process is totally foreign to a treaty. See Id., at 575-84

Third, the authority to enter into an agreement made in the name of the people cannot be politically or legally limited by any pre-existing constitution, treaty, alliance, or instructions. An agreement made in the name of a nation, however, may not contradict the authority granted to the governing powers and, thus, is so limited.

For example, the people ratified the Constitution of the United States of America notwithstanding the fact that the constitutional proposal had been made in disregard to specific instructions to amend the Articles of Confederation, not to displace them. See Sources of Our Liberties 399-403 (R. Perry ed.) (American Bar Foundation: 1972). As George Mason observed at the Constitutional Convention in 1787, "Legislatures have no power to ratify" a plan changing the form of government, only "the people" have such power. 4 The Founders" Constitution, supra, at 651

As a direct consequence of this original power of the people to constitute a new government, the Congress under the new constitution was authorized to admit new states to join the original 13 states without submitting the admission of each state to the 13 original states. In like manner, the Charter of the United Nations, forged in the name of the "peoples" of those nations, established a new international government with independent powers to admit to membership whichever nations the United Nations governing authorities chose without submitting such admissions to each individual member nation for ratification. See Charter of the United Nations, Article 4, Section 2. No treaty could legitimately confer upon the United Nations General Assembly such powers and remain within the legal and political definition of a treaty.

By invoking the name of the "peoples of the United Nations," then, the Charter of the United Nations envisioned a new constitution creating a new civil order capable of not only imposing obligations upon the subscribing nations, but also imposing obligations directly upon the peoples of those nations. In his special contribution to the United Nations Human Development Report 2000, United Nations Secretary-General Kofi Annan made this claim crystal clear:

> Even though we are an organization of Member States, the rights and ideals the United Nations exists to protect are those of the peoples. No government has the right to hide behind national sovereignty in order to violate the human rights or fundamental freedoms of its peoples. <u>Human Development Report 2000</u> 31 (July 2000) (Emphasis added.)

While no previous United Nations' secretary general has been so bold, Annan's proclamation of universal jurisdiction over "human rights and fundamental freedoms" simply reflects the preamble of the Charter of the United Nations which contemplated a future in which the United Nations operates in perpetuity "to save succeeding generations from the scourge of war...to reaffirm faith in fundamental human rights...to establish conditions under which justice...can be maintained, and to promote social progress and between standards of life in larger freedom."

Such lofty goals and objectives are comparable to those found in the preamble to the Constitution of the United States of America: "to...establish Justice, insure domestic tranquility, provide for the common defense, promote the general welfare and secure the Blessings of liberty to ourselves and our posterity..."

There is, however, one difference that must not be overlooked. The Constitution of the United States of America is a legitimate constitution, having been submitted directly to the people for ratification by their representatives elected and assembled solely for the purpose of passing on the terms of that document. The Charter of the United Nations, on the other hand, is an illegitimate constitution, having only been submitted to the United States Senate for ratification as a treaty.

Thus, the Charter of the United Nations, not being a treaty, cannot be made the supreme law of our land by compliance with Article II, Section 2 of Constitution of the United States of America. *Therefore, the Charter of the United Nations is neither politically nor legally binding upon the United States of America or upon its people.*

Even considering the Charter of the United Nations as a treaty does not save it. The Charter of the United Nations would still be constitutionally illegitimate and void, because it transgresses the Constitution of the United States of America in three major respects:

> (1) It unconstitutionally delegates the legislative power of Congress to initiate war and the executive power of the president to conduct war to the United Nations, a foreign entity;
> (2) It unconstitutionally transfers the exclusive power to originate revenue-raising measures from the United States House of Representatives to the United Nations General Assembly; and,
> (3) It unconstitutionally robs the states of powers reserved to them by the Tenth Amendment of the Constitution of the United States of America.

IV. The Charter of the United Nations Unlawfully Delegates Congressional and Presidential War Powers

Article 43 of the Charter of the United Nations requires "all Members…, in order to contribute to the maintenance of international peace and security, undertake to make available to the Security Council, on its call and in accordance with a special agreement or agreements, armed forces, assistance and facilities … necessary for the purpose of maintaining international peace and security."

To make sure that the president did not act unilaterally to place United States armed forces under United Nations command "to maintain or restore international peace and security," the United States Congress passed the United Nations Participation Act of 1945. That act provides that no United States armed forces may be employed in a United Nations peacekeeping operation without the specific approval of the terms of agreement by Congress. 22 U.S.C. Section 287 (d)

At present, Congress has never entered into an Article 43 agreement; yet, presidents from Truman through Clinton have deployed U.S. troops in service to the United Nations. How can this be explained? It began with the Korean War when President Truman "committed American forces to war on U.S. authorization but without a Congressional declaration":

> A State Department memorandum claimed that as Commander in Chief the President had full control over U.S. forces and could employ them without Congressional approval to protect "the broad interests of American foreign policy." Tuomala, "Just Cause: The Thread that Runs so True," 13 Dick. J. Int'l. Law 1, 38 (1994)

So ingrained has this claim of presidential prerogative become that President George Bush remarked to the Texas State Republic Convention in Dallas, Texas on June 29, 1992, that he " 'didn't have to get permission from some old goat in the United States Congress to kick Saddam Hussein out of Kuwait.'" 28 "Weekly Comp. Pres. Doc." 1119 (June 29, 1992)

Although President Bush had only contempt for the U.S. Congress in his decision to wage war on Iraq, he assiduously courted the United Nations Security Council for support – and for good reason. Not only did President Bush need the political support of the world community, but also he sought legitimacy for his actions under the Charter of the United Nations.

According to Article 2 (4) of the Charter of the United Nations, members are required to "refrain in their international relations from the threat or use of force against the territorial integrity or political independence of any state, <u>or in any other manner inconsistent with the Purposes of the United Nations</u>" (Emphasis added.)

According to Article 39 of the Charter of the United Nations, "the Security Council," not individual states or collections of states, "determine(s) the existence of any threat to the peace, breach of the peace or act of aggression" by any state and the United Nations Security Council, not any individual states or collections of states, alone "decide(s) what measures shall be taken," including the use of force, "to maintain or restore international peace and security."

Article 51 of the Charter of the United Nations allows for only one exception; national self-defense "if an armed attack" has occurred against a member, and even then, the member state must defer to the United Nations Security Council once it steps in with "measures necessary to maintain international peace and security." In short, the national interests of a member state must always be subordinate to the collective interests of the members, as determined by the United Nations Security Council.

Without question this subordination of America's national interests to those of the world community as determined by the United Nations Security Council is an unconstitutional delegation of the legislative power to declare war and the executive power to conduct war. As Cornell University government professor Jeremy Rabkin observed in 1998, "the Constitution presumes American sovereignty." Rabkin, <u>Why Sovereignty Matters,</u> supra, at 12

As Joseph Story wrote over one hundred years earlier: "A treaty to change the organization of the government, or annihilate its sovereignty, to overturn its republican form, or deprive it of its constitutional powers, would be void; because it would destroy, what it was designed merely to fulfill, the will of the people." II J. Story, <u>Commentaries on the Constitution,</u> Section 1508 (5th ed. 1891) Such views follow logically from the text of Article VI which states that, while the Constitution of the United States of

America is per se the supreme law of the land, only treaties "made...under the authority of the United States" may be the supreme law. As Henry St. George Tucker wrote at the turn of the twentieth century:

> The supremacy herein declared of the Constitution forbids the treaty-making power to annul any of its provisions. Its supremacy would not permit the treaty power to abrogate or annul other powers granted to any branch of the Federal Government. The long list of enumerated powers granted by this instrument to the Congress cannot be absorbed or annihilated by the treaty-making power because these powers, being parts of the Constitution, are supreme under Article VI. H. St. G. Tucker, <u>Limitations on the Treaty-Making Power Under the Constitution of the United States</u> Section 70 (Little, Brown, Boston: 1915)

According to Article I, Section 8 of the Constitution of the United States of America, it is Congress, not the president – and certainly not the United Nations Security Council – that has been granted the power to initiate the use of armed force in pursuance of American foreign policy. The president may only use such armed force in response to an imminent threat of invasion (See generally, Tuomala, "Just War," supra, at 30-35, 41-45), for Congress alone has the power:

   (1) to define and punish Piracies and Felonies committed on the high Seas, and Offenses against the Law of Nations;

   (2) to declare war, grant letters of Marque and Reprisal, and make Rules Concerning Captures of Land and Water;

   (3) to raise and support Armies;

   (4) to provide and maintain a Navy;

   (5) to make Rules for the Government and Regulations of the land and naval forces; and,

   (6) to make all Laws which shall be necessary and proper for carrying into Execution the foregoing Powers...

This amalgamation of congressional powers designed to initiate the use of armed force – whether it be a little or a lot – in the service of America's national interests in foreign affairs cannot be delegated by treaty to any foreign government or entity. Yet that is exactly what the United States Senate did in 1945 when it ratified the Charter of the United Nations and that is exactly what the Congress did when, subsequent thereto, it enacted the United Nations Participation Act.

In the United States Senate debate over both the Charter of the United Nations and the enabling act, a minority of senators contended that Chapter VII of the Charter of the United Nations constituted an unconstitutional delegation of congressional war powers because the articles contained in Chapter VII generally conferred upon the United Nations Security Council authority to initiate armed force to maintain the international peace and security, and because Article 43 specifically obligated the United States of America to participate in such armed-force initiatives. See Stromseth, "Rethinking War Powers: Congress, the President, and the United Nations," 81 Georgetown L. J. 597, 601-03, 614-18 (1993).

In response, a bipartisan United States Senate Majority contended that the only authority conferred upon the United Nations Security Council was the limited used of force in the form of a "police action," not full-scale mobilizations constituting a "war." Id. 81 Georgetown L. J. at 607-12

Pursuant to this distinction between "police action," on the one hand, and "war," on the other, Congress enacted the United Nations Participation Act of 1945 authorizing the president to negotiate an agreement with the United Nations Security Council, making a limited number of American armed forces, after approval by Congress, available for the United Nations Security Council to use as it sees fit under Article 42 of the Charter of the United Nations. Id. at 614-18

Only a handful of senators dissented. Senator Burton Wheeler of Montana warned his colleagues that "we are fooling ourselves and fooling the people of the country when we say that we will give to the President power to put down aggression with a small force, and not at the same time delegate to him the full power to declare war at any time." 91 CONG. REC. 11, 393 (1945)

> Senator Wheeler's warning soon proved prophetic. Within five years after enactment of the United Nations Participation Act, without the approval of Congress, President Truman launched a full-scale war in Korea, under the aegis of the United Nations Security Council. To justify his end run around Congress, the president called the Korean War a "police action." Had there been no Charter of the United Nations or any United Nations Security Council, President Truman would have had no political or legal ground on which to stand. As Ohio Senator Robert Taft proclaimed, "the Korean situation is changed by the obligations into which we have entered under the Charter of the United Nations." 96 CONG. REC. 9323 (1950) Indeed, the very idea that the employment of armed force in the name of the United Nations could be called a "police action" was totally dependent upon the premise that the Charter of the United Nations created a new world-wide government entity with jurisdiction to use armed force, governed by the same rules that apply to a single nation's domestic police force.

As international legal scholar, Jeffrey Tuomala, has written, however, "there is no constitutional basis for distinguishing between police actions and war." Tuomala, "Just War," supra, 13 Dick. J. Int'l. Law at 38. It is, therefore, constitutionally impossible for Congress to retain its various war power initiatives and concur with Article 42 of the Charter of the United Nations, even if the United Nations Participation Act is complied with, because Article 42, by design and effect, confers congressional power to initiate war upon the United Nations Security Council.

Not only is such a conferral an unconstitutional delegation of legislative power to initiate war, but it is an unconstitutional delegation of the president's exclusive power to act as the commander in chief of the armed forces of the United States of America and to appoint officers, with the advice and consent of the United States Senate, to exercise the executive power of the United States of America.

On May 3, 1994, President William Clinton signed Presidential Decision Directive 25 (PDD-25), a policy directive outlining the administration's position on reforming multilateral peace operations. One of the purposes of PDD-25 is to clarify United States' policy regarding command and control of United States' military personnel participating in multilateral peacekeeping operations, including those under chapters VI and VII of the Charter of the United Nations. In order to preserve the president's role as commander in chief, and at the same time to permit the placing of American armed forces under United Nations' command, PDD-25 attempts to distinguish between "command" – defined as "the authority to issue orders covering every aspect of military operations and administration," and "operational control" – defined as a "subset of command" limited to "the authority to assign tasks to United States units led by United States officers," but excluding the authority to alter the composition of units, discipline personnel, confer promotions, redistribute supplies, separate units or to "change the mission or deploy U.S. forces outside the area of responsibility." In making this distinction between "command" and "operational control," the Clinton administration hoped to avoid the claim that by placing United States military personnel under the command of a foreign government military officer, the president would no longer be the commander in chief of the United States military personnel so assigned.

The office of commander in chief, however, requires the president to be both in command and in operational control. The office contemplates that the president could "take actual command over troops in the field," as well as "to direct the movements of the armed forces, even to the extent of ordering them to deploy outside the United States in time of peace." Thus, "all phases and aspects [of] control over U.S. forces is vested [by the Constitution of the United States of America] in the president." J. Snyder, "'Command' versus 'Operational Control': A Critical Review of PDD-25," p. 6) Therefore, the president may delegate "operational control" only to officers who are accountable and responsible solely to the president. That can be assured only if the officer in "operational control" of troops in the field has sworn an oath to uphold the Constitution of the United States of America, not one to uphold the Charter of the United Nations, as is the case of United Nations commanders in the field who are, after all, ultimately accountable to the United Nations' secretary general. "Operational control," then is not "merely a 'subset of command,' but an inseparable component of it which cannot be relinquished because of the break in the chain of accountability." Id.

Such a break in the chain of command not only results from "the command structure employed in traditional peacekeeping operations" of the United Nations, but from the "collective security scheme envisioned by Article 43 and Article 47" of the Charter of the United Nations:

> Once called by the Security Council for service in an enforcement action, forces pledged under an Article 43 agreement would come under the political and strategic control of the Security Council, which would then be responsible for the strategic and political decisions regarding the use of those forces.

Although PDD-25 attempts to put a wedge between the United Nations Security Council and the president by authorizing the

United States officer commanding the unit of United States military personnel to submit a request to the president to countermand a United Nations commanders' order, nonetheless such authority is tantamount only to a veto of that order. The president cannot – under the PDD-25 policy or under the Charter of the United Nations – act affirmatively, having relinquished that authority to the United Nations secretary general and the United Nations Security Council. Hence, deployment of United States armed forces – even under the PDD-25 directive – fails to preserve the full constitutional powers of the president as commander in chief. For as the United States Supreme Court observed in Fleming v. Page, 50 U.S. [9How.] 603, 615 (1850), the president as commander in chief is "authorized to direct the movements of the naval and military forces placed in his command, and to employ them in the manner that he may deem most effectual..." [Emphasis added.]

It is true that, as commander in chief, the president need not personally exercise all of the powers conferred upon him. But he may only delegate those powers to executive officers appointed in accordance with the procedures prescribed in Article II, Section 2 of the Constitution of the United States of America that requires military officers be appointed with the advice and consent of the United States Senate. Weiss v. United States, 510 U.S. 163 (1994) Such a constitutional requirement is designed to ensure that the military be operated in such a manner as to be politically accountable to the American people through their elected representatives. Just as the Constitution of the United States of America does not permit Congress "to shift burdens and responsibilities of federal programs on the states," it does not permit the president to shift his burdens and responsibilities on foreign entities, including the United Nations and its officials. Otherwise, presidential accountability is diminished, thereby undermining the constitutional principle of vesting all the executive power in a single executive officer. Printz v. United States, 521 U.S. 898, 936-37 (1997); J. Rabkin, Why Sovereignty Matters, supra, at 18-20.

V. The United Nations General Assembly Has no Lawful Power to Require the United States to Pay Dues to the United Nations

Since the mid-1980's, the Congress of the United States of America has sometimes refused, and only reluctantly paid, its dues and other mandatory obligations to the United Nations. During this period, the United States grew increasingly weary of paying 25% of the United Nations' regular budget, not to speak of the additional monies spent on United Nations peacekeeping operations, while at the same time it had only one vote in the United Nations General Assembly, the body responsible for developing the United Nations' budget. Finally, having extracted promises of cost reductions and other budget reforms, including the formulation of the regular budget by consensus instead of a two-thirds vote, Congress appropriated nearly a billion dollars to pay its arrears and current obligations. Even if these promised reforms and budget cutbacks are affected, they will not cure the constitutional defect in the process by which the dues and other mandatory obligations of the United States to the United Nations are determined.

According to Article 17 (1) of the Charter of the United Nations, the United Nations General Assembly has the final authority to "approve the budget of the Organization" According to Article 17 (2) of the Charter of the United Nations, the United Nations General Assembly also determines the assessment upon each United Nations member to meet the expenses of the organization. Finally, according to Article 19 of the Charter of the United Nations, any member state "which is in arrears in the payment of its financial contributions to the Organization shall have no vote in the General Assembly if the amount of its arrears equals or exceeds the amount of the contributions due from it for preceding two full years, unless the General Assembly is satisfied that the failure to pay is due to conditions beyond its control." [Emphasis added.] The "basic fiscal law of the Organization," then, is that, under Article 17, the United Nations General Assembly makes the dues assessment obliging each nation to pay a certain amount in dues, and noncompliance with that assessment automatically triggers the penalty set forth in Article 19. <u>The U.N. Charter Commentary,</u> supra, at 295, 305-13, 327-39

Currently, the United Nations General Assembly calculates the assessment to be exacted upon a member state according to the member's "capacity to pay," subject to a cap of 25% of the United Nations' regular budget. Id., at 309-10 To determine that "capacity," the United Nations General Assembly takes into account "the aggregate of national income, that is, the totality of the national production of goods and services..." To "prevent anomalies in the assessment resulting from statistics," however, the United Nations General Assembly considers a number of other factors, including "comparative per-head income," "ability of members states to secure foreign currency," comparative level of economic development and "state indebtedness," Id., at 309

In essence, the United Nations' assessment system is comparable to a graduated national income tax, with deductions authorized for certain national expenditures and outstanding obligations. And while this tax does not fall individually upon the citizens of each member state, it is measured, in part, by "the comparative per-head income" of the citizens of each member states, resulting in a higher assessment imposed upon states whose citizens have a relatively high personal income, other factors of national indebtedness and state of economic development not withstanding. In other words, the assessment by the United Nations General Assembly constitutes an indirect tax upon the people of each member state, not just upon the state itself.

As a "revenue raising" mechanism, the current United Nations' mandatory dues assessment process violates Article I, Section 7, Clause 1 of the Constitution of the United States of America which provides that "All Bills for raising Revenue shall originate in the House of Representatives...." What this means is that it is the United States House, and only the United States House, which is authorized to make the initial decision to raise revenue to support the programs and operations of the United States government. Article 17 of the Charter of the United Nations, by design and effect, transfers that initiative power from the United States House to the United Nations General Assembly insofar as revenues are to be raised to support America's participation in the programs and operations of the United Nations. This unconstitutional transfer of the power to originate revenue-raising bills to support the United States involvement in the United Nations has had significant legal and political consequences.

Legally, although Congress may refuse to appropriate funds in the amount of the "tax" determined by the United Nations General Assembly, it would do so at the risk of losing United States voting rights in the United Nations General Assembly. According to Article 19 of the Charter of the United Nations, such voting rights are automatically lost upon noncompliance with its terms. This automatic penalty was placed in the charter specifically to remedy a serious shortcoming of the League of Nations. "considerable arrears [having] accumulated" for nonpayment of the member obligations which could only be enforced by "diplomatic ways and means." Id., at 295, 328; see generally, Galey, "Reforming the Regime for Financing the United Nations," 31 Howard L. J. 543 (1988)

Congress politically risks moral disapprobation if it fails to pay its "debts" to the United Nations. This moral risk has proved sufficient to persuade many members of Congress and the American People that the United States must pay its "U.N. debt arrearage, notwithstanding lingering doubts about the prospects of a "reformed" United Nations. In contrast, Congress or the President may suspend with comparative ease the United States "voluntary contributions" to United Nations programs funded outside the regular budget established by the United Nations General Assembly. For example, the Reagan administration, with relative impunity, unilaterally discontinued United States voluntary contributions to UNICEF on grounds that its activities did not conform to the foreign policy goals and objectives of the United States.

There is, however, more at stake than just the potential legal and political fallout stemming from United States resistance to United Nations monetary importunities. By permitting the United Nations General Assembly to decide how much the United States owes, the Charter of the United Nations undermines a bedrock principle of the American republic – "no taxation without representation." In the beginning, America's founders resisted the imposition of a tax upon the American people imposed by the English Parliament because Parliament was not composed of any representative elected by the people of the English colonies in the New World. Resting upon the Magna Carta, then over 560 years old, America declared her independence as a sovereign nation because King George III and the English Parliament insisted on taxing the American people without their consent.

Today, like the 18th century English Parliament, officials that are not elected by the American people form the United Nations General Assembly. Yet, like that English Parliament, the United Nations General Assembly insists that it has the right to impose upon the American people tax assessments to support policies adopted by that assembly. It is time to return the power to tax the American people for support of the United Nations to the United States House of Representatives and United States Senate that, alone, are composed of the elected representatives of the American people. In light of Article 17 of the Charter of the United Nations, there appears to be only one way to accomplish this objective: complete withdrawal from the United Nation by the United States of America.

VI. Charter of the United Nations Unconstitutionally Usurps Power Reserved to the States by the Tenth Amendment

From the outset, the Charter of the United Nations has embraced goals and objectives that, if implemented, transfer powers reserved to the states by the Tenth Amendment of the Constitution of the United States of America. The Charter's preamble, for example, does not limit the "ends" of the charter to the maintenance of international peace and security among the nations of the world, but extends the reach of the U.N. to the "employ[ment[[of] international machinery for the promotion of economic and social advancement of all peoples." To that end, the Charter of the United Nations contains an entire chapter (Chapter IX) of articles providing for the establishment of international agencies to promote worldwide economic, social, health, cultural, and educational policies. See Articles 55-60. Chapter X of the Charter of the United Nations additionally provides for the creation of the Economic and Social Council within the United Nations organization similarly to promote a worldwide agenda of economic, social, health, cultural and educational policies. See Articles 61-72.

In response, the United States government over the years has voluntarily cooperated in these international efforts, notwithstanding their adverse impact upon the exercise of traditional powers exercised by the state and local governments. Congress, for example, has appropriated hundreds of millions of dollars to support the United Nations Environment Fund, has authorized United States membership in the United Nations Educational, Scientific, and Cultural Organization, and the World Health Organization without consideration of the constitutional limitations upon congressional powers in these subject matter areas. Such wholesale delegation of power to influence domestic health, welfare and safety policy cannot be justified under the treaty power set forth in Article II, Section 2 of the Constitution of the United States of America. As Joseph Story observed in his Commentaries on the Constitution:

> ...[T]hough the [treaty] power is...general and unrestricted, it is not to be so construed as to destroy the fundamental laws of the State. A power given by the Constitution cannot be so construed to authorize a destruction of powers given in the same instrument...A treaty to change the organization of government, or annihilate its sovereignty, to overturn its republican form, or deprive it of its constitutional powers, would be void; because it would destroy, what it was designed merely to fulfill, the will of the people. II J. Story, <u>Commentar-</u>

ies on the Constitution Section 1508 (5th ed. 1891); Accord, H. St. G. Tucker, <u>Limitations on the Treaty-Making Power,</u> supra, at Sections 85-87

Twice recently, the United States Supreme Court has addressed the question of constitutionally reserved state powers in response to congressional legislation pursuant to grant of power over interstate commerce contained in Article I, Section 8 of the Constitution of the United States of America. On the second occasion, In <u>United States v Morrison,</u> —U.S.—, 146 L Ed 2d 658 (2000), the high court ruled that Congress could not, under the guise of regulating interstate commerce, usurp traditional state power to prohibit rape when such conduct is not, by nature, "economic." Otherwise, Chief Justice William J. Rehnquist contended, "Congress might use the Commerce Clause to completely obliterate the Constitution's distinction between national and local authority.." Id., 146 L Ed 2d at 674

If Congress cannot constitutionally draw on its power to regulate interstate commerce to enact laws against rape, may it rely upon the Charter of the United Nations to do so?

After all, freedom from rape has now been designated in the United Nations <u>Human Development Report 2000</u> as necessary to ensure the internationally recognized human right of "Freedom from fear – with no threats to personal security." Indeed, according to the July 2000 United Nations' report, "security from physical violence" is the most "vital" security condition necessary to realize all other human freedoms. <u>U.N. Human Development Report 2000</u>, supra, at 4.

Surely, if Congress may not use the commerce clause to completely obliterate the constitution's distinction between national and local authority, the president and the United States Senate ought not be able to use the treaty power to completely obliterate the Constitution of the United States of America's distinction between international and local authority. Yet, that is precisely what the President and United States Senate did in 1945 by negotiating and ratifying the Charter of the United Nations; the purpose of which – if honored – would obliterate all distinctions between international and domestic matters. Congress did precisely that when it authorized United States' membership in the United Nations Educational, Scientific and Cultural Organization which purports to exercise jurisdiction over "the minds of men" to the end that they might be "constructed" in such a way as to bring about international peace and security. See 22 U.S.C. Section 287m and preamble to the constitution of the United Nations Educational, Scientific, and Cultural Organization.

Although it may be true that international peace and security depends upon the minds of men, as the constitution of the United Nations Educational, Scientific, and Cultural Organization states, there is no more foundational constitutional liberty protected by the First Amendment of the Constitution of the United States of America than the following: no government has jurisdiction over the minds of individual human beings. That is the legacy of Thomas Jefferson and James Madison; the latter the chief architect of the Bill of Rights. As Jefferson put it in his 1786 "Statute Establishing Religious Freedom:"

> Almighty God hath created the mind free...[but] that the impious presumption of...rulers, civil as well as ecclesiastical, who, being themselves but fallible and uninspired men, have...set...up their own modes of thinking as the only true and infallible, and as such endeavor[ed] to impose them on others, [thereby] establish[ing] and maintain[ing] false religions over the greater part of the world and through all time.

> It is time for this Congress to return to these time-honored American principles of liberty; not to put their hope in the promise of some international organization like the United Nations which would replace the Constitution of the United States of America with its Universal Declaration of Human Rights, thereby compromising American liberties in favor of government-imposed pro-

grams designed to enhance the economic and social well-being of peoples all around the world. See generally UN Human Development Report 2000.

VII. Conclusion: HR 1146 – The American Sovereignty Restoration Act of 2001 is the Only Viable Solution to the Continual Abuses by the United Nations

By repealing (1) the United Nations Participation Act of 1945; (2) the United Nations Headquarters Act; (3) the United Nations Educational, Scientific, and Cultural Organization Act; (4) the United Nations Environment Program Participation Act of 1973; and (5) the World Health Organization Act, the Congress of the United States of America will remedy its earlier unconstitutional action embracing the Charter of the United Nations.

By terminating any further appropriations of funds to pay for (1) assessed or voluntary contributions to the U.N.; (2) contributions to any United Nations military operation; (3) contributions to any United Nations peacekeeping or peace enforcing operation; (4) contributions to support any United States armed forces or other personnel serving under the command of or auspices of the United Nations and the use of any United States facility or property by the United Nations, Congress will remedy its earlier unconstitutional authorizations of disproportionate spending of the American people's money to support governments whose national interests are diametrically opposed to the United States of America.

Finally, by directing the President to terminate United States' participation in the United Nations, including any organ, specialized agency, commission or affiliated body, by instructing the president not to grant diplomatic immunity for foreign United Nations; employees, and by requiring the president to terminate all United States' participation in all conventions and/or agreements with the United Nations, the United States will be set free to establish foreign and domestic policies in the national interest free from compromising foreign entanglements. Thereby, the United States take the advice of her first president, George Washington, who cautioned his countrymen to "steer clear of permanent alliances with any portion of the foreign world," lest the Nation's security and liberties be compromised by endless and overriding international commitments. (End of the analysis)

George Washington left these words of warnings in his "Farewell Address" when he completed his two terms as the President of the United States.

> "One method of assault may be to effect, in the forms of the Constitution, *alterations which will impair the energy of the system, and thus to undermine what cannot be directly overthrown...*"

This is exactly what the U.N. Charter does. It makes alterations to the U.S. Constitution and thus it undermines the Constitution, which cannot be directly overthrown.

Chapter 15
Conclusion

As I read the open letter from Herbert W. Titus, it made me think of the pioneers of this country who founded a new nation based on a republic type government. On June 21, 1788, Alexander Hamilton made a speech in which he said:

"It had been observed that a pure democracy if it were practicable would be the most perfect government. Experience had proved that no position is more false than this. The ancient democracies in which the people themselves deliberated never possessed one good feature of government. Their very character was tyranny; their figure deformity."

Hamilton also said on another occasion:
"We are a Republic Government. Real liberty is never found in despotism or in the extremes of Democracy."

Samuel Adams gave some insight of a democracy:
"Remember, Democracy never lasts long. It soon wastes, exhausts and murders itself! There never was a democracy that did not commit suicide."

Harrington, a British statesman, defined a republic to be, "A government of laws and not of men."

In a republic its very structure requires that both the people and their rulers obey the same basic laws and that the laws could not be changed without great effort in forming the change in the very structure of that government (the constitution).

The founders of this Nation knew very well the meaning of the word democracy and the shortcoming attached to democracies. They did everything in their power to avoid the pitfalls of a democracy.

> John Marshall, the Chief Justice of the Supreme Court 1801–1835, said, "Between a balanced republic and a democracy, the difference is like that between order and chaos."

The liberals of our day promote socialism, thinking it's the most correct type of order for a people to live by. I know socialism appeals to the *idealism* of intellectuals, that's why some school teachers, college professors, journalists and others of high intellectual ability are pro-activists for Socialism.

However, from the standpoint of human liberty, socialism has been a catastrophe. In fact, the famous scholar Alexis De Tocqueville staked his life on liberty.

"I have a passionate love for liberty, law and respect for rights."

The word democracy is not mentioned in the Declaration of Independence, and does not appear in the U.S. Constitution or in any of the State Constitutions.

It has been said "democracies are prone to war, and war consumes them."

Although it did not meet the requirements of a treaty, the United Nations Charter was adopted as a "treaty" in 1945, at which time Harry S. Truman signed on behalf of the United States.

The United Nations Charter as a "treaty" did not qualify as a treaty because it calls for General and Complete Disarmament of the United States. Any instrument of any sort or kind, which calls for the elimination of the Nation's common defense systems, is a gross violation of imperishable principles of liberty.

The United Nations itself was not a sovereign government at the time the "treaty" was prepared and ratified. On this basis alone, the so-called "treaty" could be declared "null and void." Years later on March 19, 1970, the U.N. declared itself to be a sovereign government.

At the time the U.N. Charter was ratified as a "treaty" (July, 1945), the proponents of world government began the move from theory into implementation of the world government systems. The United Nations organization had set itself up as a parallel government assisted by advancements gained through the use of Executive Orders of the President of the United States, additional "treaty" agreements, and legislative acts of the United States Congress.

No treaty can lawfully supercede the principles of the U.S. Constitution, nor the confirmed endowments of the Creator embodied in the Bill of Rights.

One U.N. "treaty" calls for the complete disarming of every American citizen. This destroys the function of the militia (the people at large) even though it is commanded in the Second Amendment of the Bill of Rights.

> No nation can survive after its common defense has been seized by a foreign power and its citizens have been disarmed.

Keep in mind also that a "treaty," if it meets Constitutional requirements, is enforceable upon every individual.

No withdrawal rights are written into the U.N. Charter. To withdraw, it would be necessary for the *individual states* of the U.S. to initiate an action demanding that the United Nations Charter *and* the United Nations Participation Act of 1945 *and* the 1949 Amendments thereto be revoked, rescinded, and repealed.

One of the goals of the proponents of the U.N. Charter is to weaken the Federal Constitution so slowly that the people will adapt and not object to the switch-over; therefore, the parallel government will ultimately remain as the only government.

As Mr. Titus states in his open letter, some would have the

people of LaVerkin believe that their city council has no authority to act to protect their residents from the unconstitutional and illegal acts of the United Nations. They claim that the President and the Congress have "preempted" the LaVerkin City Council because the United Nations is a matter of foreign affairs, not domestic concern.

The basis for the U.N.-Free Zone Ordinance is to make a statement to this Nation, to the President of the United States, to the U.S. Congress, and every Governor of the 50 States that the United States Constitution is the Supreme Law of the Land, not the United Nations Charter.

LaVerkin City got the attention of thousands of U.S. Citizens all over the country. The proof is the flood of letters and e-mails the LaVerkin City Council received after passing the U.N.-Free Zone Ordinance. Also, the Ordinance got the attention of the news media all over the world – Germany, Russia, England, and just about every major newspaper in the United States.

LaVerkin City Web Site received 2.5 million hits between July 9 and August 2, 2001. Thirty percent were outside the U.S., primarily from Canada and other English speaking countries.

The local newspaper in Washington County, in which the City of LaVerkin is located, on January 1, 2002, named the LaVerkin City's U.N.-Free Zone Ordinance as one of the top stories of the year 2001 in the State of Utah and in the Nation.

Richard Roth, a New York correspondent for CNN, reporting exclusively on the United Nations, and host of Diplomatic License, interviewed me on February 16, 2002.

I have received many requests by citizens all over this country about where to find or buy a copy of the U.N. Charter. Your bookstore can order you a 4 x 5 1/4 (105 page) book published by the Department of Public Information, United Nations N.Y.10017. The full title is *Charter of the United Nations and Statute of the International Court of Justice.*

Every U.S. Citizen should read this document.

If those who come after decide to repeal the Ordinance, then the future of LaVerkin will be of their doing for generations to come.

The citizens of LaVerkin must never allow any future City Council to repeal this safeguarding Ordinance.

It must be remembered that the Utah State Constitution Article I, Section 2 states: All political power is inherent in the people; and all free governments are founded on their authority for their equal protection and benefit, and they have the right to alter or reform their government as the public welfare may require.

The LaVerkin City U.N.-Free Zone Ordinance does involve public welfare. For it protects the citizens from the United Nations intervening in matters which are essentially within the domestic jurisdiction of the State of Utah, County of Washington, City of LaVerkin.

We must be aware that the United Nations does intervene in matters which are essentially within the domestic jurisdiction of the United States Government, as well as its state governments.

For example, the United Nations World Court found the United States in fault for violating the international rights of two German born brothers executed in 1999 and ordered the United States government to reconsider convictions in any similar cases. The International Criminal Court condemned the State of Arizona, and ruled against the United States of America.

The decision was binding and may not be appealed. If this is not intervening in matters which are essentially within the domestic jurisdiction of the United States, then I don't know what is. Walter and Karl LaGrand had been found guilty of killing a bank manager in a 1982 robbery in the State of Arizona and were executed by Arizona State Law in 1999.

Another very personal issue for LaVerkin

The United Nations at its Earth Summit in Rio 1992, adopted Agenda 21, which, among other issues, deals with freshwater protection. It calls for the regulation on the amount of water withdrawn annually from both groundwater and surface water sources.

For agriculture and other uses, Agenda 21 states that water withdrawals "must be limited to a percentage of total annual flow." Agenda 21 also sets a percentage of water of withdrawal as an indicator of the health of biodiversity, which means the lower the percentage of water withdrawn, the healthier biodiversity.

Therefore, since LaVerkin City gets some of its water supply from the Virgin River, which starts in Zion National Park, there is a possibility that the United Nations could be given by the United States State Department a biosphere within the boundary of Zion Park, which could affect our ability to irrigate our crops, fields, trees, gardens and yards.

When we heard of the U.N.-Free Zone, we wanted to pass it as soon as possible. The Council wanted to make sure the City of LaVerkin had an ordinance in place before the United Nations declared a biosphere in Zion Park. Now it's up to the people of LaVerkin to keep it for their protection in the years to come.

In the days prior to July 4, 2001, when the Ordinance was approved, there was great excitement on both sides of the issue. The news media being Pro-U.N. did everything in their power to make the City Council look like paranoid, uneducated countryfolk. They were coming from every angle. They tried their intimidation tactics every day in news print.

No matter how hard they tried to intimidate, we were bound to stand our ground, for we knew we were doing the right thing for the citizens of LaVerkin and setting an example for the people of this great Nation.

Did it take exceptional courage for the LaVerkin City Council to pass an ordinance which protects the Constitutional rights of the citizens of LaVerkin? Yes!

About the Author

Al Snow, Sr's interest in American Government studies started at Otto Township Junior-Senior High School in Duke Center, Pennsylvania, from 1951 to 1956. History teacher Mr. Richards made American History come alive with stories about American Patriots.

Mr. Snow's favorite story was about Samuel Adams, who stood up at a meeting of Patriots and said, "I think the thirteen colonies need to be free from Great Britain." Every person at that meeting thought to themselves "Can it be done?" Their deep desire to govern themselves changed the course of history. And their story has had a major influence in Mr. Snow's stand in protecting the U.S. Constitution and the sovereignty of the United States.

When the idea of having a U.N.–Free Zone came to his attention, he thought, "LaVerkin City should stand up and be the first to say we need to be a U.N.–Free Zone."

Many individuals in LaVerkin (and in the nation) thought, "Can it be done?"

After beginning his studies in American Law and Procedure in 1967, Mr. Snow received his Bachelor of Laws Degree (LL.B.) in 1971 from LaSalle Extension University of Chicago. He also received his Business Law Certificate in 1969 at Loyola University of Los Angeles, California. In 1992 he received his certification as a Paralegal affiliate in the Association of Trial Lawyers of America.

In 1994 he received his certification as an Associate in the American Bar Association (no longer a member of the ABA).

Al Snow, Sr.

That same year he also received a Certificate of Legal Assistant and Paralegal from the Blackstone School of Law in Dallas, Texas. A Councilman of the City of LaVerkin, Utah, during 2000-2001, he has two years left in a four year term.

He has been married to Launa Marie Heiner of Los Angeles for 39 years and is a father of three daughters and four sons, and grandfather of 23 grandchildren.

Acknowledgments

I owe a great deal of gratitude to the following people for their long hours of study, research, advice, work, and commitment in making sure the United States Constitution and our Republic type of government is preserved.

Daniel New of Texas was willing to take the time to come to Utah and give the LaVerkin City Council a United Nations-Free Zone presentation on June 20, 2001. Mr. New is leading the legal battle in behalf of his son, an Army Specialist, who refused to wear a United Nations uniform in 1995. He was court-martialed and convicted of disobeying an order. The case is now being prepared for the Supreme Court.

Herbert W. Titus of Virginia, the originator of the United Nations-Free Zone Ordinance. It's great to have a friend who is so dedicated in the cause for freedom and the protection of the United States Constitution and our great country. I met Mr. Titus for the first time on July 18, 2001, when he came to LaVerkin to be by my side to answer questions as the Utah Attorney General gave his interpretation of the LaVerkin City U.N.-Free Zone Ordinance.

John R. Rarick of Louisiana, Chairman of "United States Day" Committee, Inc. His example and leadership in the field of Freedom has been a source of hope in preserving the sovereignty of our nation.

Al Snow, Sr.

Bernadine Smith of California, a top-notch researcher in the field of Constitutional Law, State Law and the Gun Laws. I want to thank you for your advice, encouragement, and help furnishing articles for this book.

Corinne N. Astin of Missouri for her monthly newsletter titled "The Cutting Edge." I appreciate the many informative articles each month.

The John Birch Society for their magazine *The New American*. For the last 25 years I have read their exceptional magazines. Much of what I know about the United Nations has come from reading them and other JBS books.

Joe H. Ferguson of Utah. Thanks for your friendship and advice. Mr. Ferguson has given many years to the cause of freedom.

Patrice St. Germain of LaVerkin, news writer for the local newspaper. The LaVerkin City Council could not have gotten out our message to the rest of the nation without your news articles.

David Linnebur of Texas for furnishing the unclassified manual "Peacekeeping and U.N. Operational Control. A Study of their Effect on Unit Cohesion." Naval Post Graduate School, Monterey, Calif., March, 1995. I appreciate your interest in what the LaVerkin City Council did on July 4, 2001.

Victor Iverson, LaVerkin City Council Member. The courage, support and your vote on July 4, and July 25, 2001 for the U.N.-Free Zone Ordinance.

Daren Cottom, LaVerkin City Council Member. I appreciate your courage, support and your vote on July 4, and July 25, 2001 for the U.N.-Free Zone Ordinance.

Mayor Dan Howard of the City of LaVerkin. Thanks for your support of the U.N.-Free Zone Ordinance.

Exceptional Profile of Courage

Donald S. McAlvany of Arizona – Editor of the *McAlvany Intelligence Advisor*. I have learned much from you and appreciate your effort to keep us up-to-date on the latest news in America.

Judge J. J. Boesel, Retired. I thank you for your masterpiece "The Unconstitutional U.N. Treaty." I have a much clearer understanding of the U.N. Charter since reading your "model legal brief," why the U.N. Treaty is unconstitutional.

Henry Lamb for your article "The U.N. and Property Rights" on July 22, 2001. www.eco.freedom.org.

Barbara Jean of KTALK Radio AM630 – The Voice of Utah, "Born on the Fourth of July" show. I appreciate you having me on your talk show. Thanks for all the articles and advice.

Clyde Snyder, Producer of "Born on the Fourth of July" show KTALK AM630 Radio. Thanks for your support.

American Policy Center in Virginia "Insider Report." Thank you for your support of the U.N.-Free Zone Ordinance of the City of LaVerkin, Utah.

The Liberty Committee, Inc. Thanks for giving me permission to use the "HR 1146 – The American Sovereignty Restoration Act of 2001" – Constitutional Analysis by Herbert W. Titus, a Legal Advisor.

Sam Mahony of Illinois. Thanks for all your support and advice.

Larry Pratt – Gun Owners of America. You're a great American. Thanks for being a great example. I appreciated your article "The U.N. vs. The U.S. Constitution"

Dr. Eugene Schroder of Colorado. Thanks for your great book *Constitution: Fact or Fiction*. I gained a great education from your documentation of the F.D.R. years and the Constitution.

Al Snow, Sr.

Lloyd E. Howard of the City of LaVerkin. Thanks for being the great Patriot for the last fifty years or more. Your example is paramount in LaVerkin, Utah.

Bud Iverson of the City of LaVerkin. You're one of my heroes when it comes to standing up for the U.S. Constitution. I appreciate your many hours in the cause of freedom.

Gilbert M. Jennings of St. George, Utah. Thanks for your support and friendship.

Ralph Epperson of Arizona. I appreciate your book *The Unseen Hand*, a great effort in making a difference. It has given me a better understanding in what I need to do for this great nation.

Congressman Ron Paul of Texas. I want you to know how grateful we all feel having you at the forefront in this battle. Thank you.

The Reform Party of the United States of America. Thanks for your great support of the LaVerkin City Council declaring the city a United Nations – Free Zone.

Committee to Restore the Constitution, a Colorado Non Profit Corporation dedicated to the cause of freedom. Archibald E. Roberts, Lt Col, AUS, retired, Director. Thank you for all your work.

The Constitution of the United States: Its Sources & Application by Thomas James Norton, Copyright 1965 by Committee for Constitutional Government, Inc., a handbook for citizens and public officials. This great textbook for Law School students during the 1960s and 70s, its sources and applications, helped me immeasurably.

And my family's support and encouragement.

Exceptional Profile of Courage

Biosphere Reserve & World Heritage Sites

United Nations Conference on Human Settlements (HabitatI), held in Vancouver, May 31 to June 11, 1976. Agenda Item 10 of the Conference Report spells out the U.N.'s official policy on land.

The Preamble says:

"Land...cannot be treated as an ordinary asset, controlled by individuals and subject to the pressures and inefficiencies of the market. Private land ownership is also a principal instrument of accumulation and concentration of wealth and, therefore, contributed to social injustice: If unchecked, it may become a major obstacle in the planning and implementation of development schemes. The provision of decent dwellings and healthy conditions for the people can only be achieved if land is used in the interests of society as a whole. Public control of land use is. Therefore, indispensable..." (www.eco.freedom.org).

Also be aware of the Biodiversity Treaty, which was written mostly by the International Union for Conservation of Nature and Natural Resources (IUCN), which is an accredited scientific advisory body to the United Nations.

United Nations World Heritage and Biosphere Programs occupying over 50 million acres of United States soil at the present time include the following: *New American Magazine* August 18, 1997 pp. 13 and 15).

BIOSPHERE RESERVE

1. Aleutian Islands
2. Beaver Creek
3. Big Bend
4. Big Thicket
5. California Coast Ranges
6. Carolinian-South Atlantic
7. Cascade Head
8. Central California Coast
9. Central Gulf Coastal Plain
10. Central Plains
11. Champlain-Adirondack
12. Channel Islands
13. Coram
14. Denali
15. Desert
16. Everglades
17. Fraser
18. Glacier
19. Glacier Bay – Admiralty Island
20. Guanica
21. H.J. Andrews Exprmntal Forest
22. Hawaiian Islands
23. Hubbard Brook
24. Isle Royale
25. Jornada
26. Konza Prairie
27. Land Between the Lakes
28. Luquillo
29. Mammoth Cave Area
30. Mojave and Colorado Deserts
31. New Jersey Pinelands
32. Niwot Ridge
33. Noatak
34. Olympic
35. Organ Pipie Cactus
36. Rocky Mountain
37. San Dimas
38. San Joaquin
39. Sequoia-Kings Canyon
40. South Atlantic Coastal Plain
41. Southern Appalachian
42. Stanislaus-Toulumne
43. Three Sisters
44. University of Michigan
45. Virgin Islands National Park
46. Virginia Coast
47. Yellowstone

WORLD HERITAGE SITES

1. Wrangell-St. Elias –NP/ Glacier Bay
2. Olympic NP
3. Redwood NP
4. Yosemite NP
5. Yellowstone NP
6. Grand Canyon NP
7. Chaco NHP
8. Cahokia Mounds Site
9. Mammoth Cave NP
10. Statue of Liberty
11. Mesa Verde NP

12. Independence Hall
13. Monticello & Univ. Virginia
14. Great Smoky Mts. NP
15. Everglades NP
16. Pueblo de Taos
17. Hawaii Volcanoes NP
18. Carlsbad Caverns NP
19. Glacier NP
20. La Fortaleza & San Juan

The United Nations at its Earth Summit in Rio 1992, adopted Agenda 21, which, among other issues, deals with freshwater protection. It calls for the regulation on the amount of water withdrawn annually from both groundwater and surface water sources.

For agriculture and other uses, Agenda 21 states that water withdrawals "must be limited to a percentage of total annual flow." Agenda 21 also sets a percentage of water of withdrawal as an indicator of the health of biodiversity, which means the lower the percentage of water withdrawn, the healthier biodiversity.

United Nations Agencies and Other International Organizations, Conventions, Resolutions and Treaties

CCITT	International Telephone and Telegraph Consultative Committee
CEDAW	Convention on the Elimination of Discrimination Against Women
CERD	Convention on the Elimination of All Forms of Racial Discrimination
CFR	Code of Federal Regulations (USA)
CITES	Convention on International Trade in Endangered Species
COLREG	Convention on the International Regulations for Preventing Collisions at Sea
COPUOS	Committee on the Peaceful Uses of Outer Space
ECOSOC	United Nations Economic and Social Council
EEC	European Economic Community
FAC	Food Aid Convention
FAO	Food and Agriculture Organization
GA Res.	United Nations General Assembly Resolution
GATT	General Agreement on Tariffs and Trade
GEMS	Global Environmental Monitoring System
IAEA	International Atomic Energy Agency
IBRD	International Bank for Reconstruction and Development (World Bank)
ICAO	International Civil Aviation Organization
ICJ	International Court of Justice
ICSC	International Civil Service Commission

ICSID	International Centre for the Settlement of Investment Disputes
IDA	International Development Association
IFAD	International Fund for Agriculture Development
IFC	International Finance Corporation
IGO	International Inter-Governmental Organization
ILC	International Law Commission
ILM	International Legal Materials
ILO	International Labour Organization
IMF	International Monetary Fund
IMO	International Maritime Organization
IOC	International Oceanographic Commission
ITU	International Telecommunications Union
IUCN	International Union for the Conservation of Nature and Natural Resources
LNTS	League of Nations Treaty Series
MARPOL	International Convention for the Prevention of Pollution by Ships
NATO	North Atlantic Treaty Organization
NGO	Non-Governmental Organization
NIEO	New International Economic Order
NPT	Non-Proliferation Treaty
OAS	Organization of American States
OAU	Organization of African Unity
PCIJ	Permanent Court of International Justice
SC Res.	United Nations Security Council Resolution
SOLAS	International Convention for the Safety of Life at Sea
TIAS	Treaties and Other International Acts Series
TNC	Transnational Corporation
UNAT	United Nations Administrative Tribunal
UNCED	United Nations Conference on Environment and Development
UNCITRAL	United Nations Commission on International Trade Law
UNCLOS	United Nations Conference on the Law of the Sea
UNCTAD	United Nations Conference on Trade and Development
UNDP	United Nations Development Programme
UNEF	United Nations Emergency Force
UNEP	United Nations Environmental Programme
UNESCO	United Nations Educational, Scientific and Cultural Organization
UN GAOR	United Nations General Assembly Official Records

UNHCR	United Nations High Commissioner for Refugees
UNICEF	United Nations Children's Fund
UNIDO	United Nations Industrial Development Organization
UNIFIL	United Nations Interim Force for Southern Lebanon
UNRWA	United Nations Relief and Works Agency
UN SCOR	United Nations Security Council Official Records
UNTS	United Nations Treaty Series
UPU	Universal Postal Union
UST	United States Treaties and Other International Agreements
WARC	World Administrative Radio Conference
WFP	World Food Program
WHO	World Health Organization
WIPO	World Intellectual Property Organization
WMO	World Meteorological Organization
WTO	World Trade Organization

This list was taken from "The United Nations and International Law" edited by Christopher C. Joyner, 1997 (pp. xx, xxi, xxii). IUCN and UNICEF were added to the above list.

Rights & Powers Within the United States Constitution

Inherent Rights
One which abides in a person and is not given from something or someone outside itself. A right which a person has because he or she is a person.

Inalienable Rights
Rights which are not capable of being surrendered or transferred without the consent of the one possessing such rights.
    For example: Freedom of speech, freedom of religion, due process, equal protection of the laws and liberty.

Liberty
A broad and flexible term for freedom, absence of restraint, or self-determination.

Statue Law
Consists of enactments passed by the legislature.

Constitutional Law
Consists mainly of prescriptions framed by a constituent assembly especially summoned for the purpose, or by other special processes, for framing constitutional provisions which prescriptions generally have no validity until they have been formally approved by the electorate by way of referendum.

Administrative Law
Body of law created by administrative agencies in the form of rules, regulations, orders, and decisions to carry out regulatory powers and duties of such agencies.

Referendum
The practice of referring measures passed by the legislative body to the voters for their approval or rejection.

Prescription
The transfer of rights in, or title to.

Constituent
A principal, one who appoints an agent or attorney. A voter or member of an electorate.

The U.S. Constitution has different powers:
1. Inherent powers   Nature of government
2. Implied powers   Implication
3. Inferred powers   The reader infers
4. Expressed powers   Powers spelled out in the Constitution
5. Resulting powers   The aggregate powers.

Inherent Powers
An authority possessed without its being derived from another. A right, ability, or faculty of doing a thing, without receiving that right, ability, or faculty from another. Powers originating from the nature of government or sovereignty. Powers over and beyond those explicitly granted in the Constitution or reasonably to be implied from express grants, for example, in the foreign policy area, the Executive's inherent powers have been held to confer authority upon the President to settle the claims of American nationals against a foreign state as part of a diplomatic agreement.

Implied Powers
The writers of the Constitution implies in certain powers in contrast to expressed, where the intention in regard to the subject matter is not manifested by explicit and direct words, but is

gathered by implication or necessary deduction from the circumstances, the general language, or the conduct of the parties.

The extent that the hearer or reader "infers" while the writer or speaker "implies."

Inferred Powers
Are the powers the hearer or reader "infers." The extent that the bearer or reader "infers" while the writer or speaker "implies."

Constitutional Powers
The right to take action in respect to a particular subject matter or class of matters, involving more or less of discretion, granted by the Constitution to the several departments or branches of the government, or reserved to the people.

Expressed Powers
Powers spelled out in the Constitution.

Resulting Powers
Powers of the federal government derived from a combination of several grants or the aggregate of powers granted to the federal government.

This clause makes the Constitution adaptable to any future or unforeseen condition not anticipated by the Founders.

This clause is referred to as the implied powers clause and also referred to as the elastic clause.

General principles of Construction: Strict versus liberal

The two great principles of Construction applicable to the powers of the United States are:
1. That it can exercise no powers except those expressly or by fair implication granted to it in the Constitution.
2. That over such granted powers it has absolute control and its legislation thereunder is paramount to all conflicting state laws.

Exclusive Powers   Denied to the State. Federal power only.

Concurrent Powers No inconsistent powers.

Reserved Powers   To the States or the People

Example:
Every police officer in the State of Utah has the right to be armed with a firearm or revolver.

What is the expressed power? To have on his or her person a firearm.
1. Every police officer can be armed with a firearm.

What is the Inferred Power? 1) To use the firearm. 2) To buy bullets for the firearm. 3) To buy any type of firearm.

What is the Implied Power? The police officer uses the firearm to keep the peace.

Legislative Power
Congress to make all laws which shall be necessary and proper for carrying out execution of the foregoing powers and all other powers vested by the Constitution.

American Constitution law differs from statute law not only as regards to its character but also in respect to its source.

Legislative Act
An alternative name for statutory law. A bill which has been enacted by legislature into law.

When introduced into the first house of the legislature, a piece of proposed legislation is known as a bill. When passed to the next house, it may then be referred to as an Act. After enactment, the term "law" and "act" may be used interchangeably.

Subjects of Constitutional Law
- The organization of the government.
- The distribution of powers among its several departments.
- The regulation of the mode of choice.
- The terms and qualifications of its principle officers.
- The fixing of the suffrage and the determination of the political rights and privileges of the citizens.

Other Definitions of Constitution
A constitution may be defined as the fundamental law of the State, prescribing the principles upon which the government is established, regulating the division of sovereign powers, and indicating to what persons each power is given and the manner in which it is to be used.

A constitution to be "the fundamental" law according to which the government of a state is organized and agreeably to which the relations of individuals or moral persons to the community are determined.

A constitution to be a "written instrument" by which the fundamental powers of government are established, limited, and defined, by which those powers are distributed among several departments for their more safe and useful exercise for the benefit of the body politic.

It goes without saying that every fully organized independent state must have a constitution or body of fundamental laws according to which its government is organized and political power exercised.

Different forms and types of Constitutions as instruments of government have been classified as cumulative or evolved, as conventional or enacted, as written and unwritten, as flexible and rigid, etc.

A cumulative or evolved constitution is one which originated mainly in custom and the prescriptions of which consist of accumulated usages, conventions, common law principles, and judicial precedents.

Enacted constitutions are those which have come into existence through deliberate enactment by an assembly, with or without a popular referendum, or which have been granted by a King, emperor, or other hereditary ruler.

An unwritten constitution is one most of whose provisions, but no means all, have never been reduced to writing or at least have never been collected and embodied in a single document. Like the cumulative or evolved type, with which it is largely identical, it consists mainly of customary rules, judicial decisions, etc. These are also known as historical or evolutionary constitutions, that is, constitutions which have developed through the accumulation of experience.

A written constitution, on the other hand, is one most of whose provisions, but certainly not all, if the constitution has attained considerable age, have been reduced to writing and formally embodied in one or more written instruments. In a written constitution, the provisions have a higher legal authority in respects to ordinary statutes than do those of an unwritten constitution. Consequently, in countries where the written type constitution prevails, the statutes must conform to the provisions of the constitution.

Compacts or Charters are not a true form of constitution, because the grantor reserves the right to revoke or amend them at will and therefore they have no permanent character. Some examples are the Charters of 1814 and 1830 by the Kings of France.

The best existing example of an unwritten constitution is that of Great Britain. The question as to whether what is called English Constitutional law is really law at all; it is said to be rather a cross between history and custom.

Electoral College

This is a subject many Americans do not yet understand.

The Founders needed to find a way to establish institutions of government that would be accountable to the public will, but in ways that systematically encouraged that will to be reflective, deliberate, and truly public-minded.

Our country was founded with a Declaration that acknowledged the duty of the people to seek justice in conformity to the laws of nature and of nature's God. Our Constitution is crafted not simply to empower public will, but to empower those expressions of public will that are *most likely to be consistent with the nation's pursuit of true justice.*

The founders understood that a government designed to respond *directly, immediately and completely to the will of the majority* would be extremely unstable. A system that awarded political power to any group achieving *simple majority status* would be vulnerable to the possibility of a *majority faction* that would not represent the good of the whole.

Regional factions, for example, might form on the basis of an interest common to residents of the region, but detrimental to the Union – such as in the period leading up to the Civil War.

Glossary

Magna Carta

The charter of English political and civil liberties granted by King John at Runnymede in June 1215. A document or piece of legislation that serves as a guarantee of basic rights.

Sovereignty

The supreme, absolute, and uncontrollable power by which any independent state is governed; supreme political authority; the supreme will; paramount control of the constitution and frame of government and its administration; the self-sufficient source of political power, from which all specific political powers are derived; the international independence of a state, combined with the right and power of regulating its internal affairs without foreign dictators; is sovereign and independent. The sovereignty of the United States is its Constitution.

Liberty

The condition of being free from restriction or control.

The right and power to act, believe, or express oneself in a manner of one's own choosing.

The condition of being physically and legally free from confinement, servitude, or forced labor.

Freedom from unjust or undue governmental control.

A right or immunity to engage in certain actions without control or interference: the liberties protected by the Bill of Rights.

Communism

A system of government in which the state plans and controls the economy and a single, often authoritarian party holds power, claiming to make progress toward a higher social order in which all goods are equally shared by the people.

Habeas Corpus

The name given to a variety of writs having as their objective to bring a party before a court of judge. The primary function of the writs to release from unlawful imprisonment.

The purpose of the writ is to test or challenge the legality of the restraints or holds on a person's liberty. The traditional purpose of the writ is to secure the release of a defendant from illegal incarceration or illegal restraint of any kind.

Treaty

A formal agreement between two or more states, as in reference to terms of peace or trade. The document in which such an agreement is set down. A contract or agreement. Negotiation for the purpose of reaching an agreement.

Treaty Law can be enforced in both Federal and your own State Courts, *only if they are constitutional*.

By definition, a treaty is a contract between or among independent and sovereign nations, obligatory on the signatories only when made by competent governing authorities in accordance with the powers constitutionally conferred upon them. I Kent, Commentaries on American Law 163 (1826); Burdick, The Law of the American Constitution section 34 (1922) Even the United Nations Treaty Collection states that a treaty is (1) a binding instrument creating legal rights and duties (2) concluded by states or international organizations with treaty-making power (3) governed by international law.

The power to make treaties is bestowed upon the United States in general terms and extends to all proper subjects of negotiation between nations.

However, a treaty to which the United States is a party is not only an international compact, but also law of the land, in which it may not override the higher law of the Constitution.

Thereby, it may not change the character of the government which is established by the Constitution nor require an organ of that government to relinquish its constitutional powers.

Genocide Treaty

The United Nations' genocide treaty was adopted in 1948. It is designed to stop the destruction of national, ethnic, racial or religious groups. The Convention on the Prevention and Punishment of the Crime of Genocide was drafted after Nazi Germany's extermination of 6 million Jews in the Second World War. Convention adherents agreed to enact laws to give it effect and to try or extradite people charged under its provisions.

The convention, which was adopted by a vote of 55-0 at a meeting of the U.N General Assembly in Paris on Dec. 9, 1948, was the crusade by a Polish Jewish professor of international law, Raphael Lemkin, who lost 49 members of his family in the Holocaust. He was also concerned about persecution of other groups of people.

The convention, in force since Jan. 12, 1951, defines genocide as the committing of certain acts with intent to destroy, wholly or in part, a national, ethnic, racial or religious group and deems it a crime under international law, whether committed in war or peace.

A party to the convention may call on U.N. bodies to take action for the prevention and suppression of acts of genocide.

In Rwanda, up to 800,000 Tutsis and moderate Hutus were killed by Hutu troops, militiamen and neighbors in 1994.

Earlier, in Cambodia, an estimated 1.7 million people were killed during the rule of the radical communist Khmer Rouge over the period 1975-79.

In 1998, a special U.N. tribunal was set up to try leaders of the Rwanda genocide. This was the first occasion the provisions of the genocide convention had been carried out by a court of law.

Jean Paul Akayesu, a Hutu former mayor of Taba commune, was found guilty of nine criminal counts, including genocide, and given a life sentence.

The genocide convention has been ratified by 127 countries. Although President Harry Truman signed it on Dec. 12, 1948, Washington did not complete the ratification process until 1988. The United States became the 99th member nation after decades of efforts to overcome objections by some senators that it compromised U.S. sovereignty.

Ratify
To approve and give formal sanction to; confirm.

Self Executing Treaty
A Treaty which is effective immediately without the need of intervening court action, ancillary legislation, or other type of implementing action.

Enabling Act or Statute
Term applied to any act or statute enabling persons or corporations, or agencies to do what before they could not. It is applied to acts or statutes which confer new powers.

Public Law
That portion of law that defines rights and duties with either the operation of government, or the relationships between the government and individuals, associations, and corporations.

Civil Law
The area of law dealing with rights and duties of private parties as individual entities to be distinguished from criminal law.

Common Law
Principles of non-statutory law reflecting the customs and usages of society and that area of law deriving from judicial decisions, as opposed to legislatively enacted statutes and administrative regulations.

Substantive Law
Law that regulates and controls the rights and duties of all persons in society. In contradiction to the term adjective law, which

means the rules of court procedure or remedial law, which prescribe the methods by which substantive law is enforced.

Rule of Law

A legal principle of general application, sanctioned by the recognition of authorities, as "the supremacy of law." For example: The U.S. Constitution

Roman Law

The concept of government creating an "artificial person" with certain characteristics having legal status has an ancient origin. During the early Roman Republic various religions, educational, and governmental groups began to develop.

Constitutional Law

One which is consonant to, and agrees with, the Constitution. For example: One which is not in violation of any provision of the Constitution (federal or state).

Equity Law

The branch of the judicial system which grants relief where there is no adequate remedy at law.

Martial Law

The military rules which sometimes supercede civil laws during periods of emergency or catastrophe.

Criminal Law

Governs the acts, committed or omitted in violation of a public law governing it.

Statute

Law created by a legislative body and approved by the executive.

Natural Law

A law higher than that which is made by mortal.

Law
Norms established by the official leaders of society.

Social Engineering
Using the law to bring about social change.

Case Law
The law that comes from decided cases.

Legislative Act
Law passed by legislature in contrast to a court-made law.

Ratification
To approve and give formal sanction to; confirm.

The affirmation by a person of a prior act, which did not bind him, but which was done or professedly done on his account, whereby the act, as to some or all persons, is given effect as if originally authorized by him.

Therefore, the Federal government, in the case of the UN Charter, felt that by the legislative act of the Congress of the United States, it was done professedly for the States as well, whereby the Legislative Act is given effect as if originally authorized by the individual states.

Note: The Fourteenth Amendment made all persons born or naturalized in the United States and subject to the jurisdiction thereof citizens of the United States and of the State wherein they reside. No State shall make or enforce any law which shall abridge the privileges or immunities of citizens of the United States; nor shall any State deprive any person of life, liberty, or property, without due process of law; nor deny to any person within its jurisdiction the equal protection of the laws.

Therefore, all citizens are subject to the Federal government because of their Federal citizenship under the 14th Amendment. This is where the Federal government gets its power over the states.

Precedent
An *adjudged* case or decision of a court considered as furnishing an example or authority for an identical or similar case

afterwards arising or similar question of law. An act or instance that may be used as an example in dealing with subsequent similar instances.

Law. A judicial decision that may be used as a standard in subsequent similar cases: *a landmark decision that set a legal precedent.*

Convention or custom arising from long practice

The Liberty Committee

It is a non-profit 501 (c) 4 organization devoted to defending and advancing liberty in the United States by working in the national legislative process. The Liberty Committee is based in Falls Church, Virginia. Founder and chairman is Congressman Ron Paul of Texas. The committee was founded in August of 1998.

Bill of Rights Day

Enacted on December 15, 1791. This day is celebrated each December 15th.

United States Day Committee

This committee founded United States Day on October 23, 1953, to provide a day for every American to reflect on the things that make America the greatest nation in the world – our divinely inspired Constitution, its Bill of Rights (individual human rights) and a free enterprise economic system that has made our prosperity the envy of every nation on earth. Our system of government and the blessing flowing therefrom should make us the leader and example of the world.

Treaty of Versailles

The dilemma for the United States was that the milder the peace the greater the American role as a future interventionist power in Europe: Germany, fighting a world coalition while having only weak allies, had been overcome only through American help. A Germany left largely intact could again become a military threat, so that once again the United States would have to intervene to decide a war in Europe for the Entente. On the other side, an all too weak Germany could easily become the prey of a France wanting to establish its own predominance over Europe. France could attack Germany before it recovered and impose its own peace on Germany. American assistance would then be needed to save Germany from France. The problem was that the United States was not prepared to assume the new responsibilities it faced as a world power. As the main creditor of the Entente, it had only a short-term interest in European stability and in French and British wealth.

Altogether, we have to consider that statesmen at Versailles had little latitude. The global war had created circumstances that even good will could not easily have changed. Recent historiography has slightly rehabilitated Wilson. He made sure that at least some compromise between his ideological goals and the more aggressive aims of the French came about. The Paris peace conference had a multitude of problems to solve: Germany was only one part of them. In the following months the Entente concluded separate treaties with Austria, Hungary, Bulgaria, and Turkey (see Eurodocs, World War I Archive: Conventions and Treaties). Versailles undoubtedly helped to compromise the new German democracy, but the reasons for its failure were more complex than the Versailles trauma. The compromise character of the peace treaty left Germany some hope for revision and ultimate repudiation. There was no need to accept a total defeat as there would be in 1945. Revision remained a distant but viable goal. Germans were determined to work for it.

League of Nations

A world organization established in 1920 to promote international cooperation and peace. It was first proposed in 1918 by President Woodrow Wilson, although the United States never joined the League. Essentially powerless, it was officially dissolved in 1946.

Reservations

Reservations merely limit the obligations of one party or both parties to the Treaty. In the case of the U.S. fifth reservation in the League of Nations, the fifth reservation allowed the U.S. veto power, which Canada did not like, since Canada did not have a veto power.

United Nations

An international organization composed of most of the countries of the world. It was founded in 1945 to promote peace, security, and economic development. An organization of independent states to promote international peace and security.

The United Nations Charter, signed June 26, 1945, created the United Nations on October 24, 1945 after the Charter had been ratified by the five permanent members of the Security Council – China, France, the USSR, the United Kingdom, and the United States.

The President, by and with the advice and consent of the Senate, shall appoint a representative and a deputy representative of the United States to the United Nations, both of whom shall have the rank and status of envoy extraordinary and ambassador plenipotentiary.

Your bookstore can order you a 4 x 5 1/4 (105 page) book published by the Department of Public Information, United Nations N.Y.10017. The full title is *Charter of the United Nations and Statute of the International Court of Justice*.

Trygve Halvdan Lie

The Secretary-General of the U.N. from 1946 to 1952 was Trygve Halvdan Lie, born on 16 July 1896, in Oslo, Norway. He was educated at Oslo University where he obtained a law degree in 1919. On 1 February 1946, Mr. Lie was elected the first Secretary-General of the United Nations.

Dag Hammarskjold

Dag Hjalmar Agne Carl Hammarskjööld (pronounced HAMmar-shold) was born in 1905, the son of the Prime Minister of Sweden. He studied law and economics, and taught economics at the University of Stockholm. He became president of the board of the Bank of Sweden, then Minister of State, then head of the Swedish delegation to the United Nations, and then Secretary General of the United Nations. In 1960 the Belgian Congo (now

Zaire) became independent, and civil war promptly broke out. Hammarskjööld went in to negotiate a cease-fire, and was killed in a plane crash in Zambia on 18 September 1961.

Korean Conflict

The United Nations for the first time since its founding reacted to aggression with a decision to use armed force.

The United States would accept the largest share of the obligation in Korea. President Truman later described his decision to enter the war as the hardest of his days in office. But he believed that if South Korea was left to its own defense and fell, no other small nation would have the will to resist aggression, and Communist leaders would be encouraged to override nations closer to U.S. shores.

The American people, conditioned by World War II to battle on a grand scale and to complete victory, would experience a deepening frustration over the Korean conflict, brought on in the beginning by embarrassing reversals on the battlefield.

Many U.S. veterans of the Korean and Vietnam wars are angry at the loss of American lives, believing that the strategies of the U.N. seemed not to focus on winning the war, but in *managing* the war.

Vietnam Conflict

In another United Nations action, John F. Kennedy (1961-1963) decided to commit American support troops to South Vietnam. Four thousand troops were sent in 1962. In 1966, more than 200,000 troops were committed to Vietnam. The United States escalated its participation in the war to a peak of 543,000 troops in April 1969.

Council on Foreign Relations

A private organization, it was formed on July 29, 1921 in New York City. Today this organization has about 2000 members who are the elite in education, finance, labor, government, business, communications, and military.

Many of the founders had been at the signing of the Treaty of Versailles after the end of World War I.

Dan Smoot, one of the first researchers to look at the CFR organization stated that its purpose was "to create a one-world socialist system and make the United States an official part of it."

Forty-seven members of the CFR were in the United States delegation to the U.N. Conference in San Francisco.

World Court
A United Nations court established to settle disputes between members of the United Nations [International Court of Justice] The seat of the Court was established at The Hague.

Statute of the International Court of Justice (Excerpts)
Article 1
The International Court of Justice established by the Charter of the United Nations as the principal judicial organ of the United Nations shall be constituted and shall function in accordance with the provisions of the present Statute.

Chapter I – Organization of the Court
Article 2
The Court shall be composed of a body of independent judges, elected regardless of their nationality from among persons of high moral character, who possess the qualifications required in their respective countries for appointment to the highest judicial offices, or are jurisconsults of recognized competence in international law.

Article 3
1. The Court shall consist of fifteen members, no two of whom may be nationals of the same state.
2. A person who for the purposes of membership in the Court could be regarded as a national of more than one state shall be deemed to be a national of the one in which he ordinarily exercises civil and political rights.

Article 4
1. The members of the Court shall be elected by the General Assembly and by the Security Council from a list of persons nomi-

nated by the national groups in the Permanent Court of Arbitration, in accordance with the following provisions.

2. In the case of Members of the United Nations not represented in the Permanent Court of Arbitration, candidates shall be nominated by national groups appointed for this purpose by their governments under the same conditions as those prescribed for members of the Permanent Court of Arbitration by Article 44 of the Convention of The Hague of 1907 for the pacific settlement of international disputes.

Article 26

1. The Court may from time to time form one or more chambers, composed of three or more judges as the Court may determine, for dealing with particular categories of cases; *for example, labour cases and cases relating to transit and communications.*

2. The Court may at any time form a chamber for dealing with a particular case. The number of judges to constitute such a chamber shall be determined by the Court with the approval of the parties.

3. Cases shall be heard and determined by the chambers provided for in this article if the parties so request.

Article 32

1. Each member of the Court shall receive an annual salary.

2. The President shall receive a special annual allowance.

3. The Vice-President shall receive a special allowance for every day on which he acts as President.

4. The judges chosen under Article 31, other than members of the Court, shall receive compensation for each day on which they exercise their functions.

5. These salaries, allowances, and compensation shall be fixed by the General Assembly. They may not be decreased during the term of office.

6. The salary of the Registrar shall be fixed by the General Assembly on the proposal of the Court.

7. Regulations made by the General Assembly shall fix the conditions under which retirement pensions may be given to members of the Court and to the Registrar, and the conditions

under which members of the Court and the Registrar shall have their traveling expenses refunded.

8. The above salaries, allowances, and compensation shall be free of all *taxation*.

United Nations Security Council

The Security Council has primary responsibility, under the Charter, for the maintenance of international peace and security. It is so organized as to be able to function continuously, and a representative of each of its members must be present at all times at United Nations Headquarters. On 31 January 1992, the first ever Summit Meeting of the Council was convened at Headquarters, attended by Heads of State and Government of 13 of its 15 members and by the Ministers for Foreign Affairs of the remaining two. The Council may meet elsewhere than at Headquarters; in 1972, it held a session in Addis Ababa, Ethiopia, and the following year in Panama City, Panama.

When a complaint concerning a threat to peace is brought before it, the Council's first action is usually to recommend to the parties to try to reach agreement by peaceful means. In some cases, the Council itself undertakes investigation and mediation. It may appoint special representatives or request the Secretary-General to do so or to use his good offices. It may set forth principles for a peaceful settlement.

When a dispute leads to fighting, the Council's first concern is to bring it to an end as soon as possible. On many occasions, the Council has issued cease-fire directives which have been instrumental in preventing wider hostilities. It also sends United Nations peace-keeping forces to help reduce tensions in troubled areas, keep opposing forces apart and create conditions of calm in which peaceful settlements may be sought. The Council may decide on enforcement measures, economic sanctions (such as trade embargoes) or collective military action.

A Member State against which preventive or enforcement action has been taken by the Security Council may be suspended from the exercise of the rights and privileges of membership by the General Assembly on the recommendation of the Security Council. A Member State which has persistently violated the principles of the Charter may be expelled from the United Nations by the Assembly on the Council's recommendation.

A State which is a Member of the United Nations but not of the Security Council may participate, without a vote, in its discussions when the Council considers that that country's interests are affected. Both Members of the United Nations and non-members, if they are parties to a dispute being considered by the Council, are invited to take part, without a vote, in the Council's discussions; the Council sets the conditions for participation by a non-member State.

The presidency of the Council rotates monthly, according to the English alphabetical listing of its member States. The Council has 15 members – five permanent members and 10 elected by the General Assembly for two-year terms. Permanent members include: United States, China, France, Russian Federations, and United Kingdom.

Each Council member has one vote. Decisions on procedural matters are made by an affirmative vote of at least nine of the 15 members. Decisions on substantive matters require nine votes, including the concurring votes of all five permanent members. This is the rule of "great Power unanimity," often referred to as the "veto" power.

Under the Charter, all Members of the United Nations agree to accept and carry out the decisions of the Security Council. While other organs of the United Nations make recommendations to Governments, the Council alone has the power to take decisions which Member States are obligated under the Charter to carry out.

Functions and Powers.
Under the Charter, the functions and powers of the Security Council are:

To maintain international peace and security in accordance with the principles and purposes of the United Nations;

To investigate any dispute or situation which might lead to international friction;

To recommend methods of adjusting such disputes or the terms of settlement;

To formulate plans for the establishment of a system to regulate armament.

To determine the existence of a threat to the peace or act of aggression and to recommend what action should be taken;

To call on Members to apply economic sanctions and other measures not involving the use of force to prevent or stop aggression;

To take military action against an aggressor;

To recommend the admission of new Members and the terms on which States may become parties to the Statute of the International Court of Justice;

To exercise the trusteeship functions of the United Nations in "strategic areas":

To recommend to the General Assembly the appointment of the Secretary-General and, together with the Assembly, to elect the Judges of the International Court.

Index

A

A New World Order 11, 33
ABA 147, 176
Abortion 48
Abramns, Lt. General Creighton W. 62
Accountable 36, 158, 159, 193
Acheson, Dean 60
Acknowledgments 177
ACLU 45, 55, 57
Adams, Samuel 14, 44, 169, 175
Administrative Agencies 38, 188
Administrative Law 37, 38, 39, 188
Affirmation 26, 199
Agenda 21 50, 51, 173, 183
Amendments 9, 25, 27, 56, 123, 148, 171
America 2, 9, 22, 23, 24, 35, 39, 42, 43, 46, 50, 51, 52, 53, 54, 60, 66, 68, 81, 83, 123, 140, 141, 144, 145, 146, 147, 148, 149, 150, 151, 154, 155, 157, 158, 159, 160, 161, 163, 164, 165, 166, 167, 173, 175, 179, 180, 200
American Bar Association 176
American Court System 16
American History 175
American life 39
American Policy Center 179
American Revolution 19, 21
Angola 62
Annan, Kofi 48, 143, 144, 150
Armenians 49
Arms Control 9, 62, 78, 120, 121, 122, 125, 126, 127, 128, 129, 130, 131, 133, 134, 137
Army 12, 13, 21, 120, 177
Article–103 56, 147
Article–108 56 148
Article–109 148
Article–110 147
Article–17 89, 160, 161, 162, 163
Article–19 160, 161, 162
Article–24 142
Article–39 153
Article–4, Section–2 56
Article–42 80, 87, 155, 156
Article–43 87, 151, 152, 155, 158
Article–47 158
Article–51 153
Article–I, Section–1 39
Article–IV, Section–3 56
Article–VI 56, 57, 58, 90, 149, 158, 162
Articles of Confederation 10, 18, 19, 21, 52, 53, 147, 149
Assistant Directors 127
Astin, Corinne N. 178
Atmosphere 12, 66, 96
Austria 73, 201
Authorization 87, 88, 142, 152, 167

B

Bangkok, Thailand 62
Barbara Jean 179
Barkley, Alben W. 78, 79
Baruch Plan 95
Baumert, Kevin 47
Belgium 60
Berlin 95, 100, 101, 102
Bilderbergers 17
Bill of Rights 9, 18, 22, 25, 45, 68, 103, 122, 166, 171, 194, 200
Biological Diversity 50
Biosphere Reserves 15, 51

209

Index

Blackstone School of Law 176
Blessings of Liberty 24, 52, 53, 150
Boden, Charles 61
Boesel, Judge J. J. 179
Bowman, Isaiah 76
Bricker Amendment 64
Bricker, John 64
British 21, 74, 169, 201
Brownsville, Texas 72
Budget 46, 129, 160, 161, 162
Buffer Zone 51
Bulgaria 201
Bureaus, Offices, and Divisons 128
Burke, Edmund 54
Burma 99, 100
Bush, George 152
Byelorussia 61

C

Cambodia 49, 99, 100, 196
Chapman College 68
Charter, U.N. 9, 15, 60, 62, 63, 81, 90, 109, 116, 146, 161, 168, 171, 172, 179
Charter, United Nations 10, 11, 28, 56, 57, 59, 63, 75, 78, 81, 82, 83, 87, 97, 170, 172, 202
Chicago Tribune 76
Child 47, 93
Children 11, 13, 14, 35, 36, 42, 45
China 49, 59, 63, 72, 76, 202, 207
Churchill, Winston 40
City Council 10, 14, 51, 52, 55, 57, 58, 172, 174, 177, 178, 180
Civil Liberties 25, 194
Civil Officers 36
Civil War 193, 203
Clark, J. Ruben, Jr 65
Cleveland, President 38
Clinton, William 15, 32, 157
Columbus 54

Commander-in-Chief 31
Commentaries 44, 45, 153, 164, 165, 195
Commerce 14, 21, 37, 165
Commercial Relations 14
Commission on Global Governance 48
Committee for Constitutional Government, Inc 180
Committee on Public Information 39
Committee to Restore the Constitution 180
Common Defense 24, 52, 53, 120, 136, 150, 171
Communism 59, 60, 195
Communist 59, 60, 61, 62, 63, 76, 99, 196, 203
Communist Party 76
Comptroller General Audit 136
Conflict of Interest 134
Congolese Government 61
Congress 19, 20, 21, 26, 33, 37, 38, 39, 40, 41, 44, 53, 54, 56, 58, 62, 64, 66, 70, 71, 73, 76, 78, 79, 80, 81, 83, 85, 86, 87, 89, 94, 120, 123, 126, 131, 137, 138, 139, 140, 141, 142, 143, 144, 149, 151, 152, 154, 155, 156, 159, 160, 162, 164, 165, 166, 167, 171, 172, 190, 199
Conscription 13
Consent of the Governed 35, 52, 140, 145
Constitution 5, 9, 10, 11, 13, 18, 19, 21, 22, 23, 24, 25, 26, 28, 34, 35, 36, 37, 38, 39, 42, 43, 44, 45, 51, 52, 53, 54, 56, 57, 58, 60, 64, 68, 81, 82, 90, 103, 120, 123, 130, 140, 141, 144, 145, 146, 147, 148, 149, 150, 151, 153, 154, 158, 159, 161, 163, 164, 165, 166,

210

Index

168, 170, 171, 172, 175, 177, 179, 180, 187, 188, 189, 190, 191, 192, 193, 194, 195, 196, 198, 200
Constitutional Convention 21, 56, 148, 149
Constitutional Duty 58
Contracts or Expenditures 133, 134
Contributions 106, 111, 160, 162, 167
Coordinaton 126, 131
Copenhagen 78
Cornerstone 11
Corwin, Edwin S. 141
Cottom, Daren 178
Council of Global Government 11, 63
Council on Foreign Relations 60, 76, 203
Country 2, 5, 11, 14, 18, 35, 36, 41, 42, 43, 51, 52, 53, 60, 86, 93, 96, 98, 99, 102, 109, 116, 124, 131, 156, 169, 172, 174, 177, 193
Countrymen 14, 141, 168
Court of Justice 12, 15, 46, 74, 79, 172, 185, 202, 204, 208
Critical Account 33
Cuba 62

D

Daliver, Louis 76
Dallas, Texas 152, 176
De facto 68
De jure 68
Death by "Gun Control" 49
Declaration of Independence 19, 36, 41, 53, 54, 56, 98, 144, 170
Declaration on Disarmament 111
Democracy 22, 23, 35, 72, 169, 170, 201
Democrats 72, 77
Denmark 60

Department of Defense 33, 131, 136
Department of State Publication–7277 16, 78, 104
Depression Era 39
Dept. of Energy 52
Deputy Director 127, 133
Deseret News 45
Dickinson, John 19
Dictatorship 23
Director 86, 120, 121, 127, 128, 129, 130, 131, 132, 133, 134, 135, 136, 137, 138, 180
Disarmament 13, 17, 48, 61, 62, 78, 91, 92, 93, 94, 95, 96, 103, 104, 105, 106, 107, 109, 110, 111, 112, 113, 114, 117, 118, 119, 120, 121, 122, 123, 125, 126, 127, 128 129, 130
Disaster Relief 29
Divine Providence 53
Domestic Tranquility 24, 52, 53, 130
Dominican Republic 62
Drug Enforcement 29
Dual Compensation Laws 134

E

Earth Summit 47, 50, 51, 173, 183
East Germany 62, 100
Economic 9, 12, 13, 39, 46, 63, 68, 84, 86, 98, 101, 126, 129, 130, 143, 161, 164, 165, 167, 184, 185, 200, 202, 206, 208
Economic and Social Council 46, 84, 164, 184
Educate the Citizenry 51
Elite 203
Emigrants 2
Encroachment 21, 52

Index

Enemies 34, 35, 42, 53, 121
Enforceable laws 38
England 54, 60, 172
English Bill of Rights of 1689 25
English Legal Tradition 25
English Parliament 163
Entangling Alliance 9, 14
Enumeration 26
Environmental 9, 12, 13, 15, 29, 33, 50, 143, 184, 186
Environmental Controls 13
Environmental Disaster Clean-up 29
Environmental Security 12, 33
Environmentalists 52
Epperson, Ralph 180
Escalating 9
Essential Principles 14
Establish Justice 24, 52, 53, 150
Estonia 62
Europe 70, 71, 200, 201
Evaluation of the Ordinance 55
Evian, France 17
Executive Agreements 40
Executive Branch 21, 37, 39, 40, 67, 125, 126
Executive Order 15, 82, 137
Extermination 71, 93, 196

F

Facts About the United Nations 59
FAO 184
Farewell Address 14, 53, 168
Federal Government 16, 19, 20, 21, 25, 63, 78, 80, 81, 82, 154, 189, 199
Federal Registry 38
Federalist Papers 45
Ferdinand 54
Ferguson, Joe H. 178
Firearms 32, 43, 44, 48, 49, 122, 123, 124
Firm Reliance 53
First Amendment 26, 166

First Stage 107
Flag 22, 35, 41, 42, 57
Food Administration 39
Food and Agriculture Organization 46, 184
Forefathers 2, 9, 22
Foreign Policy Committee 60
Fort McHenry 41
Founding Fathers 10, 123
Fourteenth Amendment 199
Fourth Amendment 26
France 17, 59, 60, 192, 201, 202, 207
Free State 26, 43
Free World 76, 77
Free Zone 10, 14, 15, 45, 52, 55, 56, 58, 172, 173, 174, 175, 177, 178, 179, 180, 210
Freedom 2, 9, 13, 14, 17, 25, 26, 35, 41, 44, 57, 62, 70, 78, 100, 101, 102, 103, 104, 105, 109, 150, 165, 166, 177, 178, 179, 180, 181, 187, 194
Friendship 14, 178, 180
Frontier Borders 20

G

General Assembly 32, 46, 56, 57, 61, 63, 84, 85, 89, 91, 93, 104, 123, 139, 140, 145, 148, 150, 151, 160, 161, 162, 163, 184, 186, 196, 204, 205, 206, 207, 208
General Welfare 24, 52, 53, 150
Geneva 71, 72, 73, 74, 96
Germain, Patrice St. 178
Germany 49, 59, 72, 73, 100, 172, 196, 200, 201
Global 11, 12, 13, 14, 15, 46, 47, 48, 50, 63, 98, 123, 143, 184, 201
Global Commons 12, 47

Index

Goodman, Sherri Wasserman 33
Government 4, 7, 10, 11, 14, 15, 16, 17, 18, 19, 20, 21, 22, 23, 25, 26, 27, 28, 29, 32, 33, 34, 35, 36, 37, 38, 39, 42, 45, 46, 48, 51, 52, 53, 54, 56, 57, 59, 60, 61, 63, 64, 66, 67, 68, 69, 70, 71, 75, 76, 77, 78, 80, 81, 82, 83, 89, 100, 103, 123, 125, 126, 127, 129, 130, 131, 132, 134, 135, 136, 137, 140, 141, 143, 145, 148, 149, 150, 153, 154, 155, 156, 157, 162, 164, 166, 167, 169, 170, 171, 173, 175, 177, 178, 180, 188, 189, 191, 193, 194, 195, 196, 197, 198, 199, 200, 203, 206
Grain Corporation 39
Great Britain 19, 74, 76, 175, 192
Greece 60
Guatemala 49
Guns 14, 43, 123, 124

H

Hamilton, Alexander 21, 169
Henry, Patrick 44, 53
Heroes 180
Hiss, Alger 60, 61, 76
Home 13, 14, 42, 53
Honest 14
House of Representatives 21, 34, 83, 85, 151, 161, 163
Howard, Dan 178
Howard, Lloyd E. 180
Hull, Cordell 60
Human Rights 9, 12, 16, 61, 63, 68, 69, 92, 143, 144, 150, 167, 200
Human Rights Treaties and Declarations 12
Humanitarian Relief 30
Hungary 62, 201

I

I Kent 145, 195
IAEA 46, 115, 184
IBRD 46, 184
ICAO 46, 185
ICC 12, 16
ICSID 46, 185
IDA 46, 185
Idealism 170
IDO 113, 114, 115, 116, 117
IFAD 46, 185
IFC 46, 185
Ignorance 37
Ignorant 24, 45
IGO 185
ILO 46, 185
IMF 46, 47, 185
Immunities 57, 66, 67, 68, 199
India 60
Individual Freedom 9, 11, 25
Individual Rights 2, 13, 17, 22, 63
Intent, True 139
Interdependent 10
International Atomic Energy Agency 46, 184
International Bank for Reconstruction and Development 46, 184
International Center for Settlement of Investment 46
International Civil Aviation Organization 46, 185
International Code of Conduct 12
International Criminal Court 12, 16, 173
International Development Association 46, 185
International Disarmament Organization 95, 106, 109, 110, 112, 113, 117
International Environmental Court 12

213

Index

International Finance Corporation 46, 185
International Fund for Agricultural Development 46
International Issue 13
International Labor Organization 46
International Monetary Fund 46, 185
International Organization Immunities Act of 1945 67
International Telecommunication Union 46
Introduction 9, 25, 29, 104, 139, 141
Isabella 54
Italy 60
ITU 46, 185
IUCN 15, 16, 181, 185, 186
Iverson, Bud 180

J

Jefferson, Thomas 14, 24, 54, 166
Jenner, William E. 28
Jennings, Gilbert M. 180
Jews 49, 196
John Birch Society 178
John F. Kennedy 91
Judicial authority 20
Judicial proceedings 20
Justice 12, 15, 22, 23, 24, 27, 35, 36, 42, 46, 52, 53, 74, 79, 105, 111, 143, 150, 165, 170, 172, 185, 193, 102, 204, 208

K

Katanga 61
Keep and Bear Arms 23, 26, 43, 44, 123
Kellogg, Frank 74
Kennedy, John F. 17, 91, 203
Kentucky 41, 78
Key, Francis Scott 41
Khrushchev, Mr. 100

King George III 163
Kissinger, Henry 17
Klamath Basis of Southern Oregon 50
Know Your Duty 45
Korean 62, 152, 156, 203
Kutakov, Leonid 62

L

Labor 9, 12, 46, 54, 73, 94, 194, 203
LaGrand, Karl 173
LaGrand, Walter 173
Lamb, Henry 179
Langer, William 61
LaSalle Extension University 175
Latvia 62
LaVerkin City 14, 16, 55, 57, 58, 172, 173, 174, 175, 177, 178, 180
Law 8, 11, 22, 26, 28, 35, 36, 37, 38, 39, 53, 54, 56, 57, 62, 63, 64, 68, 71, 77, 78, 80, 81, 82, 83, 85, 86, 87, 89, 92, 93, 97, 98, 101, 105, 109, 111, 117, 119, 120, 121, 122, 123, 124, 125, 130, 131, 132, 133, 134, 144, 145, 146, 151, 152, 154, 156, 160, 170, 172, 173, 175, 176, 178, 180, 185, 186, 187, 188, 190, 191, 192, 195, 196, 197, 198, 199, 200, 202, 204
League of Nations 60, 70, 71, 72, 73, 75, 76, 162, 185, 201, 202
League to Enforce Peace 70
Lederer, Edith M. 16
Lee, Richard Henry 44
Legal Assistant 176
Legislative Halls 36
Leopoldville 61

214

Lie, Trygve 61
Limited Powers 20, 77
Linnebur, David 178
Lithuania 62
Local Issue 13, 50, 51
Los Angeles 17, 175, 176
Loyalty 28, 41, 42, 134, 135
Loyola University 175
Lumumba, Patrice 61

M

Madison, James 21, 54, 166
Magna Carta 25, 146, 163, 194
Mahony, Sam 179
Malaysia 62
Mansfield, Mike 67
Marion, Ohio 72
Marshall, John 170
Mason, George 149
Master Plan 50
Mayan Indians 49
McAlvany, Donald S. 179
McKinley, President 38
Mexico 65
Military 9, 18, 27, 61, 62, 65, 88, 94, 97, 103, 109, 110, 116, 117, 119, 121, 122, 123, 126, 130, 132, 142, 157, 159, 167, 198, 200, 203, 206, 208
Militia 26, 43, 171
Minnesota 61
Minority 22, 23, 155
Misprision of Treason 27, 28
Monetary system 13
Monroe, President 53
Myers, Dr. Norman 48

N

Nation 10, 14, 17, 21, 23, 24, 34, 35, 36, 37, 40, 41, 42, 45, 46, 52, 53, 58, 68, 69, 78, 79, 84, 94, 95, 96, 98, 99, 102, 108, 115, 120, 121, 141, 145, 146, 148, 149, 150, 161, 163, 169, 170, 171, 172, 174, 175, 178, 180, 197, 200, 203
National 11, 12, 13, 14, 15, 16, 20, 29, 41, 42, 43, 51, 52, 53, 61, 64, 76, 82, 86, 87, 88, 92, 105, 106, 111, 121, 125, 126, 129, 130, 131, 133, 134, 136, 143, 144, 145, 146, 150, 153, 155, 161, 165, 167, 173, 182, 196, 200, 204, 205
National Building 29
National Government 11, 14, 20, 51, 53
National Guard 43
National Military Establishment 88
Nationalist China 49
Natural Resources 181, 185
NCOs 31
Negotiations and Related Functions 131
New American 47, 48, 50, 178, 182
New, Daniel 177
New Horizons 97
New World Order 11, 33, 123
New York 11, 21, 45, 54, 63, 66, 77, 91, 203
New York Times 77
Ninth Amendment 26
Non-Commissioned Officers 31
Non-Governmental Organization 15, 16, 185
Non-Territorial Seas 12
North Dakota 61
Norton, Thomas James 180

O

Oath 26, 28, 31, 34, 51, 103, 158
Off-limits to Humans 51
Ohio 64, 72, 156

Index

One Child Policy 47
One World Government 10
Organization 16, 27, 28, 36, 45, 45, 46, 56, 60, 64, 65, 67, 70, 75, 76, 77, 79, 81, 82, 83, 91, 92, 93, 94, 95, 105, 106, 109, 110, 112, 113, 117, 120, 124, 125, 126, 127, 136, 150, 153, 160, 164, 166, 167, 171, 184, 185, 186, 191, 200, 201, 202, 203, 204
Otto Township Junior-Senior High School 175
Outer Space 12, 97, 98, 108, 116, 184
Ownership of property 14

P

Paralegal 175, 176
Parents 13, 60
Paris 21, 71, 72, 76, 196, 201
Park Rangers 52
Pasvolsky, Leo 60
Patents 130
Patriots 35, 175
Paul, Ron 17, 139, 180, 200
PDD-25 157, 158, 159
Peace 1, 14, 29, 32, 34, 36, 53, 59, 60, 61, 62, 70, 73, 75, 76, 77, 87, 91, 92, 93, 94, 95, 96, 97, 98, 99, 100, 101, 102, 103, 104, 105, 106, 109, 110, 111, 112, 116, 117, 118, 119, 121, 122, 125, 126, 128, 130, 142, 143, 146, 151, 152, 153, 155, 157, 158, 164, 166, 167, 190, 195, 196, 200, 201, 202, 206, 207, 208
Peace Keeping 29
Peaceable Citizens 44
Peaceful World 17, 62, 78, 104, 105, 111

Pearl Harbor 60
Pennsylvania 175
People 2, 10, 11, 14, 17, 22, 23, 24, 26, 35, 36, 37, 38, 43, 44, 45, 46, 48, 49, 51, 52, 53, 55, 56, 57, 58, 59, 61, 62, 64, 71, 76, 97, 98, 99, 100, 101, 122, 123, 140, 143, 144, 145, 146, 147, 148, 149, 151, 153, 156, 159, 161, 162, 163, 165, 169, 170, 171, 172, 174, 177, 181, 189, 190, 193, 195, 196, 203
Per Capita Rights 12
Perfect Union 24, 35, 52, 53
Personal Automobile Ownership 13
Personal Beliefs 13
Personal Disarmament 13
Planners 47, 76
Pledge of Allegiance 22, 42
Poland 62, 75
Police Action 30, 80, 155, 156
Police Force 13, 17, 156
Policy Formulation 126, 130
Political Connection 14
Pombo, Richard 17, 139
Population Control 13
Posterity 14, 24, 35, 52, 53, 150
Poverty 13, 98
Power Flows Upward 14, 51
Pratt, Larry 179
Preamble 23, 24, 52, 56, 145, 147, 150, 163, 166, 181
Preservation of Life 44
Private Ownership 14
Private Property 13, 51, 52
Private Property Rights 13
Privileges 22, 23, 57, 66, 67, 191, 199, 206
Prohibited 26, 89, 108, 110, 116, 119
Prosper, Pierre-Richard 16
Provide for the Common Defense 24, 52, 53, 150

Index

Public Law 87-297 62, 78, 120, 121, 122, 123, 125
Pucinski, Rep. 69

Q

Questionnaire 18, 27, 29

R

Rabkin, Jeremy 143, 153
Rarick, John R. 63, 177
Raritan, N.J 73
Reagan, Ronald 103
Reforming the Regime for Financing the United Nations 162
Regulatory 38, 188
Reid v. Covert 90
Related Environment 12
Religion 13, 26, 36, 54, 187
Relinquishing 9
Republic 18, 22, 23, 25, 35, 36, 42, 45, 54, 62, 77, 152, 163, 169, 170, 177, 198
Research 55, 98, 120, 126, 128, 129, 130, 177
Resolution 61, 66, 67, 78, 86, 98, 137, 184, 185
Resources 9, 13, 48, 111, 129, 181, 185
Respectively 26, 53
Revolution 19, 21, 28, 35
Revolver 190
Richards, Mr. 175
Rights Protected 25
Rio de Janeiro 47, 50
Roberts, Archibald E. 180
Roosevelt, Franklin Delano 40, 143
Roosevelt, Theodore 38, 39
Rule of Law 35, 37, 53, 97, 105, 111, 125, 198
Russian Federations 207
Russian Revolutionary 60
Rwanda 49, 196

S

Safety of Society 36
San Francisco 60, 75, 76, 79, 204
Schroder, Dr. Eugene 179
Second Continental Congress 19, 20
Second Stage 109
Secretary General 46, 61, 92, 93, 143, 144, 150, 158, 159, 202
Secure the Blessings of Liberty 24, 52, 53, 150
Security Council 12, 46, 57, 59, 61, 62, 63, 75, 80, 83, 84, 86, 87, 142, 143, 145, 148, 149, 151, 152, 153, 154, 155, 156, 158, 159, 185, 186, 202, 205, 206, 207
Security Requirements 134
Self Defense 48
Senate 21, 40, 44, 56, 57, 61, 63, 64, 66, 67, 71, 72, 73, 74, 78, 79, 82, 83, 84, 85, 127, 128, 141, 151, 155, 157, 159, 163, 165, 166, 202
Senate Subcommittee on the Constitution 44
Servitude 14, 194
Shipping Fuels 12
Shipstead, Henrik 61
Shotwell, James T. 76
Simma, B. 145
Smoot, Dan 204
Snyder, Clyde 179
Snyder, J. 158
Social Engineering 199
Socialism 170
Socialist 47, 204
Southeast Asia Collective Defense Treaty 62
Sovereignty 5, 9, 10, 14, 15, 17, 23, 45, 55, 57, 76, 77, 82, 98, 120, 139, 140, 142, 143, 144, 150, 153, 159, 164, 167, 175, 178, 179, 188, 194, 197

217

Index

Spanish 21
Speak 160
Spirit 45, 94
St. George 15, 180
Staff Officers 133
Stalin, Joseph 40, 61, 76
Stand Up 175
Star Spangled Banner 41
Stevens, Richard W. 49
Story, Joseph 153, 164
Strong, Maurice 47
Stump, Bob 17, 139
Success 1, 37, 79
Summary 105, 139, 140
Supreme Law 56, 64, 144, 151, 154, 172
Sustainable 2, 12
Sustainable Development 12
Switzerland 72

T

Taft, Robert 156
Taxing 9, 163
Teach your Children 14
Tenth Amendment 26, 139, 140, 151, 163
Terror 92, 102
The American Sovereignty Restoration Act of 2001 140, 167, 179
The American's Creed 34
The Constitutional Stage 38
The Great Rule of Conduct 14
The Liberty Committee 55, 139, 179, 200
The New Deal Stage 39
The People 11, 14, 22, 23, 24, 26, 35, 36, 37, 43, 44, 51, 52, 53, 55, 56, 57, 58, 59, 64, 101, 122, 123, 140, 145, 146, 147, 148, 149, 151, 153, 156, 161, 163, 165, 169, 170, 171, 172, 174, 181, 189, 190, 193, 195

The Provisions of the Articles 20
The Reform Party of the United States 180
The Right to Keep and Bear Arms 13, 43, 44
The Salt Lake Tribune 16
The Supreme Court of the United States 37, 82
The Union 11, 41, 43, 53, 56, 148, 193
The United Nations Loyalty Oath 28
The United Nations Participation Act of 1945 80, 82, 83, 152, 155, 167, 171
The United Nations Today 65
The War Power Act 40
The War Trade Board 39
The World Bank 46, 47, 48
Third Stage 110
Thomas Jefferson 14, 24, 54, 166
Tibet 62
Time Magazine 11
Titus, Herbert W. 55, 139, 169, 177, 179
Tobin, James 46
Tobin Tax 12
Tocqueville, Alexis De 170
Tranquility 24, 42, 43, 52, 53, 150
Transfer of Activities and Facilities to Agency 137
Transfer of Power 9, 143
Transnational Corporations 12
Treaty 16, 21, 38, 50, 56, 62, 63, 64, 66, 67, 71, 72, 73, 78, 81, 82, 83, 95, 96, 101, 103, 107, 113, 114, 121, 123, 130, 140, 141, 145, 146, 147, 148, 149, 150, 151, 153, 154, 155, 164, 165, 170, 171, 179, 181, 185, 186, 195, 196, 197, 200, 201, 203
Treaty of Versailles 72, 200, 203

Index

Troops 17, 29, 30, 31, 95, 99, 101, 102, 142, 152, 158, 196, 203
Truman, President Harry S. 78, 152, 156, 170, 203
Trusteeship Council 46, 84
Tshombe, Moise 61
Tuomala, Jeffrey 156
Turkey 49, 60, 201
Twelve Principles 11

U

U.N. Charter 9, 15, 60, 62, 63, 81, 90, 109, 116, 146, 161, 168, 171, 172, 179
U.N. Declaration of Human Rights 61
U.N. Earth Summit 50
U.N. Headquarters 61
U.N. Soldier 31
U.S. Archives 39
U.S. Citizens 13, 15, 16, 32, 172
U.S. Code Title 18 – Crimes and Criminal Procedure 27
U.S. Combat Troops 29, 30, 31
U.S. Constitution 11, 13, 23, 36, 39, 43, 52, 90, 103, 168, 170, 171, 75, 179, 180, 188, 198
U.S. Department of State Publication–7277 16
U.S. Government 18, 32, 33
U.S. Military 27, 62
Uganda 49
Ukraine 61
Under-Developed Countries 1
Understanding 10, 52, 129, 130, 139, 179, 180
UNESCO 46, 186
UNHCR 46, 186
UNICEF 46, 162, 186
Union 11, 24, 35, 41, 42, 43, 46, 49, 52, 53, 56, 59, 61, 94, 97, 99, 100, 108, 148, 181, 185, 186, 193
Unit Cohesion 29, 178
United Kingdom 59, 95, 202, 207
United Nations Army 12, 13
United Nations Army or Police Force 13
United Nations Children's Fund 46, 186
United Nations Declaration of Human Rights 69
United Nations Educational, Scientific and Cultural 46, 186
United Nations Free Zone 14
United Nations Headquarters 167, 206
United Nations High Commissioner for Refugees 46, 186
United Nations "Human Rights" Treaties and Declaration 12
United Nations Secretary General 143, 159
United States Arms Control and Disarmament Agency 78, 127
United States Day 68, 177, 200
United States Marines 18, 29
Universal Declaration of Human Rights 166
Universal Postal Union 46, 186
Untangled 9, 14
UPU 46, 186
Use of Funds 137
USSR 59, 202
Utah 14, 15, 43, 45, 51, 55, 172, 173, 176, 177, 178, 179, 180, 190, 210
Utah Constitution 43
Utahns 45

V

Vermont 41
Versailles 71, 72, 200, 201, 204
Veto power 12, 63, 73, 202
Vietnam 30, 62, 99, 100, 203
Virgin River 16, 173
Virginia 21, 177, 179, 182, 183, 200

219

Index

Vote 9, 15, 20, 22, 61, 63, 64, 66, 67, 72, 73, 78, 101, 148, 160, 178, 196, 207

W

Warrants 26, 43
Wars of Liberation 99
Washington 14, 51, 53, 79, 143, 172, 173, 197
Washington, George 14, 21, 49, 90, 141, 168
We The People 24, 37, 52, 53, 56, 147
Weakness 21, 42, 93
Weapons 43, 44, 48, 49, 50, 93, 95, 96, 97, 98, 102, 103, 104, 106, 108, 110, 111, 112, 114, 115, 116, 117, 118, 121, 122, 123, 124, 129
Welfare 24, 52, 53, 79, 143, 146, 150, 164, 173
Western Allies 101
Western Powers 101
Western Territories 20
Westmoreland, Gen. William 62
Wheeler, Senator Burton 155
WHO 46, 186
Wilson, President Woodrow 39, 70, 71, 72, 73, 201
Wisdom 92
WMO 46, 186
World 1, 7, 8, 10, 11, 13, 14, 15, 16, 17, 32, 33, 39, 40, 44, 45, 46, 47, 48, 50, 51, 53, 56, 59, 60, 61, 62, 63, 64, 66, 68, 69, 70, 71, 72, 73, 74, 75, 76, 77, 78, 79, 83, 92, 93, 95, 96, 97, 98, 100, 102, 103, 104, 105, 106, 109, 110, 111, 118, 119, 120, 121, 122, 123, 125, 128, 141, 146, 152, 153, 156, 163, 164, 166, 167, 168, 171, 172, 173, 181, 182, 185, 186, 196, 200, 201, 202, 203, 204
World Court 16, 46, 63, 64, 73, 74, 121, 173, 204
World Habeas Corpus 69
World Health Organization 46, 164, 167, 186
World Heritage Sites 15, 51, 181, 182
World Meteorological Organization 46, 186
World Monetary 13
World Peace 1, 32, 61, 75, 77, 128
World Trade Organization 46, 64, 186
World War I 39, 70, 75, 201, 204
World War II 39, 40, 59, 60, 75, 98, 203
WTO 64, 186
WTrO 46

Y

Yale 46
Yalta 40, 41, 61
Yeltsin, Boris 103

Z

Zelman, Aaron 49
Zion National Park 15, 16, 173

You may obtain a copy of the UN-Free Zone Ordinance by contacting Al Snow, Sr.

Al Snow Sr.'s web site.
www.friendinfreedom.com

http://untreaty.un.org/ is the United Nations site and contains extensive material.

Information on how to do an ordinance is available on: www.friendinfreedom.com. Organizations devoted to American Liberty and their web sites are also listed.

A Limited First Edition hard cover of this book may be ordered from Al Snow, Sr.

Al Snow, Sr.
P.O. Box 158
LaVerkin, Utah 84745
E-mail: al@friendinfreedom.com
Voice mail or Fax: (801) 406-0213

For direct sale credit card orders call:
1 (800) 360-5284